Gatekeeping

243

COMMUNICATION CONCEPTS

This series reviews enduring concepts that have guided scholarly inquiry in communication, including their intellectual evolution and their uses in current research. Each book is designed to provide organized background reading for those who intend further study of the subject.

Gatekeeping

Pamela J. Shoemaker

SAGE PUBLICATIONS
The International Professional Publishers
Newbury Park   London   New Delhi

For information address:

 SAGE Publications, Inc.
2455 Teller Road
Newbury Park, California 91320

SAGE Publications Ltd.
6 Bonhill Street
London EC2A 4PU
United Kingdom

SAGE Publications India Pvt. Ltd.
M-32 Market
Greater Kailash I
New Delhi 110 048 India

Printed in the United States of America

ISBN 0-8039-4436-5 (c)   ISBN 0-8039-4437-3 (p)

ISSN 1057-7440

FIRST PRINTING, 1991

Sage Production Editor: Astrid Virding

Citation Instructions:

When citing a **Communications Concepts** issue, please follow this reference style:

Shoemaker, Pamela J. (1991). *Communication Concepts 3: Gatekeeping*. Newbury Park, CA: Sage.

Contents

Foreword

Each volume in the **Communication Concepts** series deals at length with an idea of enduring importance to the study of human communication. Through analysis and interpretation of the scholarly literature, specialists in each area explore the uses to which a major concept has been put and point to promising directions for future work.

In the comparatively young field of communication research, *gatekeeping* is one of the oldest and best known constructs. The term has passed readily into both scientific and popular discussions of the way messages are selected, created, and controlled. Most communication scholars are familiar with gatekeeping as a metaphor introduced by Kurt Lewin and studied empirically by David Manning White, but the linkage between that early work and related current research is not so well recognized. We asked Pamela J. Shoemaker, a social scientist noted for her studies of professional mass communicators, to bring together many current strands of theory and research in gatekeeping.

Gatekeeping, as she shows, is applicable to much more of communication research than just its original domain of news editing. The concept offers interesting insights into organizational communication and behavior and is related to recent theories ranging from the psychology of choice and decision making to the macro dynamics of ideology and social change. It is clear in retrospect that this very general applicability is what Lewin, one of the most broadly inquisitive of the early communication scholars, originally envisioned for the concept.

With the publication of Shoemaker's *Gatekeeping*, students of communication are afforded a new view of an old idea, one that can inform and enrich the study of many aspects of communication. Established lines of inquiry can be reexamined, including topics that have not been thought of as gatekeeping studies at all. As related research is reconceptualized, it will in turn give new meanings to the gatekeeping concept itself. In either event, communication scholarship will be strengthened by this stimulating theoretical excursion.

—Steven H. Chaffee, *Series Editor*
Mark Levy, *Associate Editor*

GATEKEEPING

PAMELA J. SHOEMAKER

Introduction

Simply put, gatekeeping is the process by which the billions of messages that are available in the world get cut down and transformed into the hundreds of messages that reach a given person on a given day. Gatekeeping studies have most often looked at the selection of news items within the mass media, but gatekeeping can involve more than just selection. Donohue, Tichenor, and Olien (1972) have suggested that gatekeeping be defined as a broader process of information control that includes all aspects of message encoding: not just selection but also withholding, transmission, shaping, display, repetition, and timing of information as it goes from the sender to the receiver. In other words, the gatekeeping process involves every aspect of message selection, handling, and control, whether the message is communicated through mass media or interpersonal channels.

On a more microscopic level of analysis, gatekeeping also can be thought of as the process of reconstructing the essential framework of an event and turning it into news. People who see an event occur pass along some details and not others (Schramm, 1949a). Analysts provide interpretation and can emphasize some aspects while downplaying others. Communicators pick some elements of a message and reject others. The elements selected are evaluated according to their importance, with the most important elements being displayed most prominently and presented most quickly and/or frequently. One day's news represents the

1

effects of many gatekeepers at many gates. It is probably not an overstatement to say that all communication workers are gatekeepers to some degree, for gatekeeping is an integral part of the overall process of selecting and producing messages. Not only is it impossible for everything to be transmitted, but it also is impossible to transmit something without in some fashion shaping it.

Although gatekeeping research in the field of communication has most commonly involved the mass media, the gatekeeping metaphor can be applied to any decision point involving any bit of information, whether transmission is expected to occur through mass or interpersonal channels. Schramm (1949b, pp. 175-176), for example, distinguished between "media chains" and "interpersonal chains"—both channels through which messages can pass from sender to receiver, via gatekeepers. Diffusion studies, for example, could be said to involve gatekeeping, with every person in a social system acting as a potential gatekeeper for others (Greenberg, 1964).

The usual definition of gatekeeping involves an activity performed by a communication organization and its representatives. Our discussion of gatekeeping will start at the point at which a communication worker first learns about an actual or potential message and it will stop at the point at which a subset of those messages is transmitted to a receiver. A gate is an "in" or "out" decision point, and messages come to the communication organization from a variety of channels. For example, some messages may come from routine channels (e.g., from wire services or as the result of a news beat), some may come unsolicited (e.g., press releases), and others may be sought out by a communication worker (e.g., following up a possible news story) or even created by the communication worker (e.g., investigative reporting).

The process of gatekeeping involves selecting from among a large number of messages those few that will be transmitted to one or more receivers. A message may face several "in" or "out" decisions (gates) during the gatekeeping process, and selection may operate on individual bits of information as well as on whole messages or series of messages. In addition, the nature of the selection process can affect what happens to the message once it is selected, due to "forces" around the gates (Lewin, 1951). For example, a negative force that tends to reject a message (e.g., difficulty in acquiring it) will become positive if the message is selected, thus encouraging favorable shaping, display, repetition, and timing of the message's transmission.

This process is as old as the process of communication—the town crier had to decide what to announce and what to withhold, and even gatekeeping in academic journals (the journal referee system) dates back to the mid-1600s (Ryan, 1982). In addition, gatekeeping has always been an integral part of the book publishing industry, not only determining which books get published but also influencing the content and presentation of a writer's work (Bonn, 1989). Book editors play a role similar to that of city editors on newspapers, negotiating with the author through all stages of publication including writing, editing, production, and distribution (Fensch, 1977).

In the past 50 years or so, the gatekeeping concept has attracted many communication scholars who have sought to explain the differential flow of messages throughout time and space. Most of these studies have involved mass media messages, particularly news, probably because gatekeeping has given mass communication researchers a conceptual structure for comparing media content with some other measure of "reality." Although it is commonly agreed that selection occurs as a natural part of the communication process, scholars have not agreed on whether selection results in distortion or truth. The gatekeeping approach has allowed media scholars to evaluate whether professional norms of balance and objectivity ensure against bias and distortion by showing that the selection process results in media content that somehow reflects reality (Tuchman, 1981). Donohue et al.'s (1972) extension of gatekeeping by introducing dependent variables other than selection (e.g., how prominently a message is communicated) have broadened the concept's usefulness in studying bias. For example, although it might be possible to show that liberal and conservative political candidates get about the same number of stories in the newspaper or evening television news, the liberals might be always shown in favorable photographs or the conservatives might always be given more prominent coverage, leading us to potentially very different conclusions about gatekeeping's effects on what ultimately becomes mass media content.

Although several gatekeeping models have been proposed (McQuail & Windahl, 1981), none covers the full complexity of gatekeeping in the communication process. This may help explain why O'Sullivan, Hartley, Saunders, and Fiske (1983, pp. 97-98) say that gatekeeping is "oversimplified and of little utility." Yet the concept can be discussed in more complex terms: This book will cover gatekeeping on five levels of analysis, looking at individual communicators' gatekeeping decisions, the influences of communication routines, organizational-level gatekeeping, social and institutional factors, and social system influences such as ideology and culture.

I will synthesize what is known about gatekeeping, relate it to the relevant sociological and psychological literature, and create a new gatekeeping model, presented in the final section of the book. Gatekeeping may be a well-studied concept, and perhaps well-worn, but it is hardly worn out. It can be approached from a variety of theoretical angles, and the application of new theories to its study will keep it an active idea in the literature for some time to come.

Gatekeeping is important because gatekeepers provide an integrated view of social reality to the rest of us. Although each selection event in the gatekeeping process is itself ultimately trivial, the fact that millions of selection decisions are made every day makes the gatekeeping process highly significant. Add to that the fact that each outcome of gatekeeping is transmitted to millions of people daily and the result is a conception of gatekeeping as a crucial part of the process through which political and economic elites may control culture and the rate at which culture changes. Gatekeeping is, therefore, a basic and powerful force in society. As Bagdikian (1983, p. 226) has put it, "The power to control the flow of information is a major lever in the control of society. Giving citizens a choice in ideas and information is as important as giving them a choice in politics." Hardt (1979, p. 22) writes: "Control over the media of dissemination may suggest control over the mind of society." As a result, the way in which we define our lives and the world around us is largely a product of the gatekeeping process. Influences on gatekeeping directly affect our view of social reality.

1. History of the Concept

It has always been obvious that not all information reaches us: A used car salesman may not tell everything he knows about the Ford I am about to buy, a friend may not say what she really thinks about my new hairstyle, and my local newspaper provides scant coverage of South American politics. The process of communication involves selecting some bits of information for transmission and rejecting others. As Leo Rosten pointed out in his 1937 study of Washington correspondents, "A newspaper is neither a chronology, an almanac, nor a history. . . . The entire process of journalism . . . rests upon *selection*" (p. 255). More than a decade later, Wilbur Schramm (1949a) wrote that no other aspect of communication is as impressive as the large number of selections and rejections that have to be made to form the appropriate symbol in the minds of both the communicator and the receiver.

But the selectivity inherent in the communication process lacked a theoretical focus until Kurt Lewin provided the metaphor of the gatekeeper and David Manning White gave the gatekeeper life under the pseudonym of Mr. Gates. The gatekeeper concept offered early communication scholars a framework for evaluating how selection occurs and why some items are selected and others rejected. It also provided a structure for the study of processes other than selection, that is, how content is shaped, structured, positioned, and timed.

Kurt Lewin's "Theory of Channels and Gate Keepers"

The first pairing of the terms *gatekeeping* and *communication* apparently came in the posthumous publication in 1947 of Kurt Lewin's unfinished manuscript "Frontiers in Group Dynamics: II. Channels of Group Life; Social Planning and Action Research" in the journal *Human Relations*. At the time of his death, Lewin was director of the Research Center for Group Dynamics for the

Massachusetts Institute of Technology, but he had earlier held appointments at other U.S. universities, including the University of Iowa (Marrow, 1969).

A second version of the "frontiers" manuscript appeared as part of the chapter "Psychological Ecology" in the 1951 book *Field Theory in Social Science,* an edited and synthesized collection of Lewin's work.[1] The term *field theory* refers to one half of a split in German psychology around World War I, with the concept of fields having been borrowed from physics (Bavelas, 1948). One group was in favor of breaking down the person and the environment into isolated elements that could be causally connected. Lewin, trained as a physicist, was more aligned with the other group, which "attempted to explain behavior as a function of groups of factors constituting a dynamic whole—the psychological field" (Bavelas, 1948, p. 16). The field consists of both the person and the surrounding environment. Field theorists looked at a problem in terms of the dynamic interplay between interconnected factors rather than as relationships between isolated elements. Lewin was working on a way to express psychological forces mathematically, using "geometry for the expression of the positional relationships between parts of the life space, and vectors for the expression of strength, direction, and point of application of psychological forces" (Bavelas, 1948, p. 16). Forces that shape people's behaviors could be studied quantitatively by psychologists, Lewin argued, in much the same way that forces such as gravity are studied by physicists.

Lewin's (1947b, p. 146) "theory of channels and gate keepers" was developed as a means of understanding how one could produce widespread social changes in a community, and his major examples involved changing the food habits of a population. Lewin concluded that not all members of the population are equally important in determining what is eaten and that social change could best be accomplished by concentrating on those people with the most control over food selection for the home.

Food reaches the family table through "channels," said Lewin. One channel is the grocery store, where food is purchased, but there are also other channels for food, including growing fruits and vegetables in the family garden. Figure 1.1 illustrates how channels may be subdivided into "sections." For example, in the grocery channel, the first three sections include the discovery of

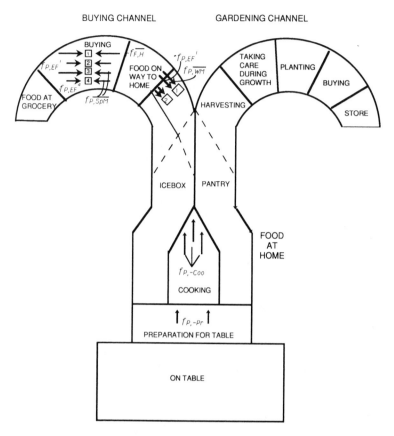

Figure 1.1. Kurt Lewin's (1951, p. 175) model of how food passes through channels on its way to the table.

food at the grocery store, the purchase decision, and transporting the food home. Food traveling along the garden channel begins with the seeds or plants available in a garden store and their purchase and planting. As the fruits and vegetables grow, some literally will be weeded out, some will be consumed in the garden by insects or children, and others may die from lack of fertilizer or water. Of the final selection of fruits and vegetables available to the household, only some will be harvested; others will languish on the vine or branch. At this point, food from the grocery channel merges with food from the garden channel, and a storage decision must be made (in the refrigerator or pantry?) for each food unit. Some foods may be "lost" in the deep recesses of the refrigerator or pantry, and others may be wasted because they were incorrectly stored (does an opened jar of peanut butter have to be refrigerated?). Next, the cook must decide whether (and how) to cook the food or to pass it immediately through to the next section, preparation for the table. The final section is the placement of the food on the family table, where it may be consumed (Lewin, 1947b, p. 144). At every stage, a food unit may be rejected or accepted, and part of the acceptance process may entail a change in the food (e.g., potatoes become fried or baked).

The entrance to the channel and to each section is a "gate," and movement within the channel is controlled by one or more "gatekeepers" or by a set of impartial rules (Lewin, 1951, p. 186). For example, some food never gets into the grocery channel because of the buying decisions or policies of the store manager/gatekeeper, and each shopper/gatekeeper may see only part of the food items that the grocery offers on a given day. From among those items that the shopper sees, some items will be bought and others rejected. Although most purchased food will be transported successfully to the household, part of it may be eaten along the way and some perishables may be ruined in transit. Once in the home, the gatekeeper evaluates where the food should be stored, whether it should be cooked, how it should be prepared, and ultimately whether to put it onto the table.

A key to Lewin's analysis was realizing that there are different forces acting on the selection of a unit, such as a food item, in different parts of the overall channel. When the shopper considers a food item for purchase in the grocery, there are both positive and negative forces acting on its selection. For example, attractiveness tends to encourage purchase, whereas expense tends to constrain it. Once the food item has passed through the purchase gate, however, previously negative forces become positive and begin to facilitate movement of the item through subsequent gates. For example, the decision to buy an expensive cut of meat may be difficult, because the decision is constrained by the high cost of the meat—"It's so expensive; should I buy it?" Once bought, however, these same forces work to ensure that the meat will be successful in getting through all other gates and reaching the table—"It's so expensive; I must take extra care to transport, store, cook, prepare, and serve it carefully and well." Because the forces before and following a gate are different, whether a unit passes through the channel depends on what happens at each gate in the channel.

In Figure 1.1, arrows show how forces act to facilitate or constrain the passage of items either within a channel section or on both sides of a gate. Forces are designated in italics; for example, $f_{P,EF}{}^1$ represents the force associated with the attractiveness of the food within the section "buying," and it should facilitate the food's passage through the next gate into the "food on way to home" section. Other forces are also present within the buying section, however, such as the force $f_{P,EF}{}^2$, which represents the expense of the food item. As Figure 1.1 shows, the high-expense force yields to a countervailing force against spending money, $f_{P,SpM}$, and thus it is unlikely that the food item will pass through to the next section. Foods that do get into the "on way to home" section leave it with a force against wasting money, $f_{P,WM}$, which helps ensure that the food passes into the appropriate icebox or pantry section.

Lewin believed that this theoretical framework could be applied generally:[2]

> This situation holds not only for food channels but also for the traveling of a news item through certain communication channels in a group, for movement of goods, and the social locomotion of individuals in many organizations. A university, for instance, might be quite strict in its admission policy and might set up strong forces against the passing of weak candidates. Once a student is admitted, however, the university frequently tries to do everything in its power to help everyone along. (Lewin, 1951, p. 187)

Although the terms *channel, section,* and *gate* imply physical structures, it is clear that they are not objects at all but represent a *process* through which some units pass on their way, step by step, from discovery to use. Sections correspond to events or states of being that occur in the channel. Gates are decision or action points. Gatekeepers determine both which units get into the channel and which pass from section to section. They may exercise their own preferences and/or act as representatives to carry out a set of preestablished policies.

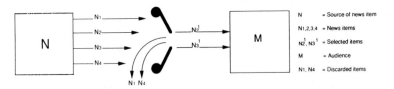

Figure 1.2. David Manning White's version of gatekeeping (from McQuail & Windahl, 1981, pp. 100-101). Used by permission.

David Manning White and "Mr. Gates"

The first communication scholar to translate Lewin's theory of channels and gatekeepers into a research project was David Manning White, who learned about Lewin's work while serving as his research assistant at the University of Iowa. White persuaded a wire editor on a small-city newspaper—whom he called "Mr. Gates"—to keep all of the wire copy that came into his office from the Associated Press, United Press, and International News Service during one week in February 1949. Mr. Gates also agreed to provide written explanations of why each of the rejected stories was not used—and about 90% of the wire copy received was not used. This allowed White to compare the stories actually used with the aggregate of stories that the wire services transmitted during the week.

The selection decisions, according to White (1950, p. 386), were "highly subjective." About a third of the time, Mr. Gates rejected stories based on his personal evaluation of the merits of the story's content, especially based on whether he believed the story to be true. The other two thirds of the stories were rejected because there wasn't enough space for them or because other similar stories had run or were already running.

Figure 1.2 presents McQuail and Windahl's (1981, pp. 100-101) version of White's gatekeeper model. News sources (N) send news items to the media gatekeeper, which turns some away (e.g., N_1 and N_4) and sends others (N_2^1 and N_3^1—the superior numerals indicating that the news items may be changed as they pass through the gate) on to the audience (M). Figure 1.2 could be interpreted to indicate only one gatekeeper or a set of gatekeepers that act in concert. The model is limited in that it does not recognize that multiple gatekeepers may each have their own role conceptions or positions in the gathering, shaping, and transmission of news.

A 1966 replication of White's study by Paul Snider—with the original Mr. Gates—yielded much the same result. Although Mr. Gates was 17 years older and had only one wire service instead of three from which to choose, his story selections were still based on what he liked and on what he thought his readers wanted. He used fewer human interest stories in 1966, whereas he used more international war stories, showing more of an interest in hard news. When asked how he defined news, Mr. Gates said: "News is the day by day report of events and personalities and comes in variety which should be presented as much as possible in variety for a balanced diet" (Snider, 1967, p. 426).

Other Gatekeeping Models

White's study stimulated many others, and, by 1965, Webb and Salancik considered the gatekeeping literature one way in which "journalism research has moved appreciably toward a more rigorous approach to data" (p. 595). In one of the first of these studies, Gieber (1956) looked at 16 newspaper telegraph editors' selections of wire copy, and his conclusion was very different than White's. Whereas White concluded that the gatekeeper's personal values were an important determinant of selection, Gieber (1956, p. 432) described the editor as being "caught in a strait jacket of mechanical details" that keeps personal values from having a major influence on the selection of stories. Gieber (1964, p. 175) proposed that personal subjectivity was not as important a factor in gatekeeping as "the number of news items available, their size and the pressures of time and mechanical production." The wire editor, said Gieber (1956), is essentially passive, and the selection process is mechanical. Gieber saw the organization and its routines as more important than the individual worker in shaping the gatekeeping process.

A year later, Westley and MacLean (1957) proposed a model of mass communication that combined the idea of gatekeeping as an organizational activity with Newcomb's (1953) ABX coorientation model. (Westley had been Newcomb's student.)

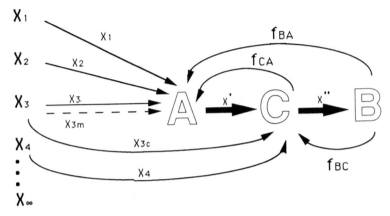

Figure 1.3. Westley and MacLean's (1957, p. 35) model of the mass communication process, showing "C" as the gatekeeper. Used by permission.

Newcomb proposed the idea of coorientation—two people simultaneously orienting toward each other and an object—as a way of studying communicative acts. He saw every communicative act as involving the transmission of information about an object; the simplest model involved person A sending information about object X to person B.

Westley and MacLean expanded this idea by adding C to represent the mass media channel (the organization as gatekeeper), using the character X to designate individual messages, and designating "feedback" by the letter f (Westley & MacLean, 1957, p. 35). Arrows in Figure 1.3 show the flow of messages (whether news items or feedback) from one actor to another. The introduction of C into the ABX model means that not all messages that could flow between A and B are in fact transmitted to B. Some are waylaid by C, the mass media gatekeepers. Westley (1953, p. 332) saw news judgment as the essential explanation of gatekeeping decisions.

Figure 1.3 shows multiple bits of information (each represented by an X) going to the media channel C, some through the source A and some directly to C. As in White's model, not all information bits are successful in passing through the media channel to the audience. B receives some subset of the messages available to C and may provide feedback both to C and to A about the messages. In their extension of Newcomb's model, Westley and MacLean point out that, at any given point in time, there are multiple As, Bs, and Cs, whose dyads communicate via the mass media.

White's approach to the study of gatekeeping differs in an important way from the approach taken by Gieber and by Westley and MacLean. Whereas White's study focused on the decisions of one person, Gieber's study and Westley and MacLean's model treat the media organization as monolithic, with individual workers collectively acting as one gatekeeper. Gieber's (1956) study of 16 wire editors emphasized that it was not the individuals' attributes or attitudes that were important but the organizational constraints imposed on the individual. The organization or channel in Westley and MacLean's (1957) model is another example. Individual communication workers are unimportant in the Gieber and Westley and MacLean approaches: Individuals are passive and have no important distinguishing features; they are interchangeable cogs in the media machine. White, on the other hand, looked at gatekeeping as a process performed by people, not organizations. He saw individual decisions being influenced both by the individual's characteristics and values and by organizational constraints such as deadlines.

Later studies again pick up the idea of individuals acting as gatekeepers. McNelly (1959, p. 25) proposed a model that showed how international news items pass through multiple individual gatekeepers on their way from the source to the audience. As Figure 1.4 shows, a story (S) is written about an event (E). The story passes from one gatekeeper (C) to another, each of whom may cut, reorganize, or merge it with another story before it ultimately reaches the receiver (R). Gatekeepers included foreign correspondents, editors, "rewritemen," "deskmen," and telegraph and/or radio or television news editors. McNelly (1959, p. 23) wrote that "a piece of news destined for a foreign audience typically must run an obstacle course of reportorial error or bias, editorial selection and processing, translation, transmission difficulties, and possible suppression or censorship." Another innovation of the McNelly model was in showing how new items may enter subsequent gates (e.g., item S_2 in Figure 1.4), either to displace existing items or to be integrated with them. Dotted arrows represent feedback, which McNelly says is infrequent.

14

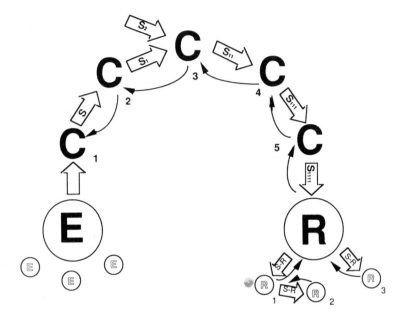

Figure 1.4. McNelly's (1959) expanded model shows how a message passes through multiple gates. Used by permission.

Bass (1969) also looked at individuals as gatekeepers but, in his approach, only the individual's job within the news organization is of interest. The individual acts as a representative of the organization in fulfilling certain functions necessary to the flow of news within the organization. Bass argued that not all news gatekeepers perform the same type of gatekeeping function, and he produced yet another model (Figure 1.5) to show the two primary functions that result in "double-action internal newsflow" (Bass, 1969, p. 72). *News gatherers,* according to Bass, take the information (raw news) that comes to them from various channels and turn it into news copy. News gatherers have job titles such as writers, bureau chiefs, reporters, or city editors. (Although Bass suggests that his model would hold for both the print and the broadcast media, his examples are from newspapers.) A second type of gatekeeper—the *news processor*—modifies and integrates the copy into a finished product that can be transmitted to the

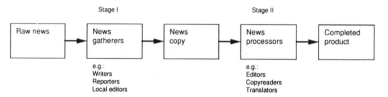

Figure 1.5. Bass's (1969) model recognized that not all gatekeepers perform the same function; he divided the process into news gatherers and news processors. Used by permission.

audience. News processors include editors, copyreaders, and translators. Thus Bass broadened the study of individual gatekeepers from White's study of one news processor to the study of multiple gatekeepers of two distinct types.

In a similar argument a year later, Halloran, Elliott, and Murdock (1970, p. 131) wrote that gatekeeping begins not in the office (with the news processors) but with the "reporter on the street" (the news gatherer) and that the extent to which editorial staff act as gatekeepers varies between newspapers. Chibnall (1977, p. 6) disliked the terms *gatherer* and *processor* because they imply that news exists independently of the media: "The reporter does not go out gathering news, picking up stories as if they were fallen apples, he *creates* news stories by selecting fragments of information from the mass of raw data he receives and organizing them in a conventional journalistic format." News is constructed from a variety of raw materials, the most important of which comes from sources; reporters rarely use their own direct experience in covering an event. Chibnall argues that the journalist-source nexus is the most important arena of gatekeeping. By the time the story gets to an editor, the most important gatekeeping decisions have already been made: "Events have occurred, they have been experienced, accounts of experiences have been constructed for particular audiences, accounts of those accounts have been fashioned and these have either been stored away or transformed into full-fledged news stories. At every stage selection and processing has taken place" (Chibnall, 1977, p. 7).

In some cases, however, the materials that come to the journalist are not so raw. As Gandy (1982) has pointed out, one role of the public relations industry is to provide "information subsidies" that are in a form attractive to and easily used by the media. In such cases, much of the gathering and processing has occurred before the item comes to the attention of the journalist/gatekeeper. This increases the likelihood that the item will be selected to pass a media gate. News gatekeepers can thus include not only news gatherers, sources, and news processors but also public relations practitioners and other representatives of interest groups who want to shape mass media content.

Gatekeeping and the General Communication Process

The concept of gatekeeping has proven to be popular with mass communication scholars, particularly in the study of news selection. Gatekeeping has clear applicability to entertainment programming as well (Cantor, 1980), but it has not been as popular with those who study interpersonal communication. According to Hirsch (1977, p. 21), this may reflect the

> larger role and institutional function of journalism in a democratic society more than it signals differences between constant categories at the production level, for a discovery that news editors' selection criteria are subject to personal bias and political pressure suggests more significant implications for public policy.

We do, however, see parts of the gatekeeping metaphor applied to interpersonal communication. For example, in their study of communication among members of small groups, Bales, Strodtbeck, Mills, and Roseborough (1951) used the term *channel of communication* to refer to interaction between any two members of a group or between any member and the group as a whole. Their interest was not in the selection of items to be communicated but in what the distribution of communications among channels revealed about the relative power of group members.

In his study of formal channels and power within an organization, Hickey (1966, 1968) identified three types of organizational information control: through (a) a communication handler, who controlled the passage of messages within an organization; (b) a channel mediator, who controlled the nature of the channels or networks through which information could pass; and (c) a content manipulator, who could perform both of the other two roles plus shape the nature of the content. All of these roles represent types of gatekeeping, with the content manipulator having the most power. In Hickey's network analyses, combinations of five people were asked to solve a problem. One person was in the center of the network, acting as a gatekeeper for the four people around the periphery. Hickey showed that the person with the most topological centrality—seen in terms of the control of information, for example, by a gatekeeper—was accorded the highest status in the group and was perceived as being the most powerful. Hickey (1966, pp. 106-107) suggests that Lewin (1947) and White (1950) viewed gatekeeping from the vantage point of the gate, dwelling on whether the gate was open or closed, whereas a more productive interpretation might include perceptions of the gatekeeper by others in the field and the gatekeeper's own reactions toward the status of the job.

Another interpersonal approach to the study of gatekeeping could include theories of cognitive heuristics (e.g., Kahneman, Slovic, & Tversky, 1982; Nisbett & Ross, 1980). The "representativeness heuristic"—automatic assignment of an item to a category based on its similarity to other items in the category—can be applied to the gatekeeper's assessment of whether a message should be selected or rejected. For example, Tuchman (1974) showed that journalists assign events to several categories, such as hard or soft news, to organize an otherwise uncontrollable job—handling the flood of information that is presented to them each day. If a story is deemed representative of the hard news category, it would be treated quite differently than if determined to be soft news. We will return to the topic of cognitive heuristics in more detail in a later section on the individual level of analysis.

The gatekeeping metaphor has also been compared with that of *boundary role persons* in the organizational communication literature (e.g., Adams, 1980). Boundary role persons are those who interact with other organizations and outside people, controlling those messages (for example) that both come into and leave the organization. This aspect of gatekeeping is covered in a later section on the organizational level of analysis.

In addition, research on the diffusion of information is applicable to gatekeeping: Gatekeepers can facilitate or constrain the diffusion of information as they decide which messages to allow past the gates and which to stop, making them important actors in the diffusion process. As Chaffee (1975) points out, the factors that constrain and facilitate diffusion are the most interesting to study because they result in diffusion patterns that deviate from the standard S-shaped (normal) curve found in many studies. If gatekeepers constrain the flow of information, it may not completely diffuse throughout a social system, whereas if they facilitate information flow, news of the event may diffuse more quickly. Because news may diffuse both through interpersonal and through mass media channels, even "ordinary" people may be gatekeepers for others. But not all individual gatekeepers are equally powerful; those who represent the mass media control the diffusion of information for millions of people, a fact that gives them extraordinary political power.

Notes

1. Lewin had previously written about gatekeeping and "channel theory" in a 1943 government research report, "Forces Behind Food Habits and Methods of Change," for the National Research Council, but the report did not generalize the gatekeeping process to communication items, as did his 1947 manuscript.

2. Legend has it that Lewin and Wilbur Schramm shared a backyard fence when both were at the University of Iowa and that they hoed weeds and talked about theory by the hour. Perhaps these conversations were the inspiration for Lewin's suggestion that gatekeeping could be applied to the study of communication.

2. The Gatekeeping Process

Antecedents of Gatekeeping

In this section, we will explore factors that determine which items come to the attention of communication workers. These include factors influencing the entrance of items into the channel, the nature of forces in front of and behind the gates, gatekeepers' personal attitudes and values, journalists' role conceptions and type of job, and characteristics of the items.

Entrance of items into the channel. Gatekeeping begins at the point at which information is created or discovered by a communication worker. Where does the pool of items or messages come from? Some come knocking and others have to be dragged kicking and screaming through the gate. Information comes to communication organizations through a variety of channels. Sigal (1973, p. 120) categorizes these as routine, informal, and enterprise:

> *Routine* channels include (1) official proceedings such as trials, legislative hearings, and election tabulations; (2) press releases as well as reports monitored over official radio or from TASS; (3) press conferences, including daily briefings by "official spokesmen" and broadcast interviews, and (4) nonspontaneous events, such as speeches, ceremonies, and staged demonstrations. *Informal* channels include (1) background briefings; (2) leads; (3) nongovernmental proceedings like association meetings or trade union conventions; and (4) news reports from other news organizations, interviews with reporters, and newspaper editorials. *Enterprise* channels include (1) interviews conducted at the reporter's initiative; (2) spontaneous events which a reporter witnesses firsthand, like fire, riots, and natural disasters; (3) independent research involving quotations from books and statistical data; and (4) the reporter's own conclusions or analysis.

Routine and informal channels bring information to the communication organization from the outside, where a boundary role person (Adams, 1980) makes the first in/out decision. Many sources—for example, government officials or public relations practitioners—create their own messages and work to ensure that they will enter media channels and pass through all gates. They create messages that are particularly attractive to the communication worker, hoping that a message's attractiveness will create positive forces in front of a gate that will facilitate its movement past the gate. (This idea is developed more fully in the following section.)

Information coming through enterprise channels is either initiated and developed by the communication worker (e.g., reporter-initiated interviews) or a result of the communication worker being in the right place at the right time when an event (e.g., a fire) occurs naturally in the environment. In the former case, sources may alert the mass media of some events or journalists may experience them firsthand. A journalist who deems the item sufficiently newsworthy will allow it past the first gate and into the media organization. For example, a reporter learns that a public official is to be charged with a crime, and an editor gives instructions to the reporter to go out and gather more information. In the latter case, journalists may be on hand when an event occurs, thus bringing the event to the first gate themselves. This was the case with the 1989 central California earthquake, which was given immediate media coverage because national journalists were already at work covering a World Series baseball game and experienced the earthquake firsthand. Investigative journalists, on the other hand, develop their own stories by tying disparate ideas and events together into a logical whole, cajoling reluctant sources and uncovering a story that might not have come to light on its own (Ettema, 1988). The classic example is Woodward and Bernstein's (1974) investigation of the Watergate scandals, which caused U.S. President Richard M. Nixon to resign.

In Sigal's study of the *New York Times* and the *Washington Post*, most information came through routine channels, with about half of the items from the U.S. government, indicating the influence that officials—particularly those from government—have in composing the queue of news items at the first gate into the medium.

Although there are billions of possible messages that *might* come to the attention of communication workers, the vast majority never make it to the first gate. They may be trivial for the society at large and not judged by any source to be worth promoting, for example, a child's school report card. Other messages may not be seriously considered because they represent normal conditions; unusual or deviant events are most likely to be reported (Shoemaker, Chang, & Brendlinger, 1987). For example, the normal efficient and ethical work of government officials gets no media coverage, whereas a questionable or inefficient action can generate protracted public debate. Even the fact that a journalist personally experiences an event does not ensure its entrance through the first gate. If nothing important happened at the Planning Commission meeting last night, no story is likely to be filed.

Limitations of the human senses exert another constraint on the entry of messages into a media channel. Some events are invisible to most of us, such as the movement of subatomic particles, and others may occur without human witnesses, such as the proverbial tree falling in an empty forest. Even when there are witnesses, their accounts and interpretations of what they have seen may differ widely. When considering the same event, one person may interpret it as trivial and usual, whereas another may consider it newsworthy. Only the latter witness would bring the event to the attention of the first media gatekeeper.

In addition, some gatekeepers may be influenced by actions of previous gatekeepers. For example, Whitney and Becker (1982) suggest that newspaper editors tend to select news items in roughly the same proportion as they were received from wire services. Hirsch's (1977) and McCombs and Shaw's (1976) reinterpretations of White's (1950) study suggest that Mr. Gates's selections were more influenced by what the wire services sent him than by his own opinions. This might mean that many gatekeepers' work is not very important—if a person merely follows someone else's lead in the proportion of stories to include in several categories of news, then that person is exercising selection within each category but not between them. We will return to this idea in the section on gatekeeping at the organizational level of analysis.

Other gates may be "low" or "easy" to pass, as Judd (1961, pp. 40-41) found in his study of a newspaper that tried to include "something for everyone." A message is probably more likely to be published by a newspaper that has a relatively small pool of messages from which to choose than by a newspaper with more options. Likewise, the number of news items available on weekends is generally smaller than those between Monday and Friday, resulting in some items being selected on the weekend that would be rejected on another day.

Characteristics of the items. Some messages are clearly more newsworthy than others, and the more newsworthy a message is, the more likely it is to pass a news gate. What kinds of information are most newsworthy? There are many lists of newsworthy attributes, and they generally include some or all of the following: timeliness; proximity; importance, impact, or consequence; interest;

conflict or controversy; sensationalism; prominence; novelty, oddity, or the unusual (Dennis & Ismach, 1981; Harriss, Leiter, & Johnson, 1977; Izard, Culbertson, & Lambert, 1973; Stephens, 1980).

Nisbett and Ross (1980, pp. 43-62) take a more general cognitive approach to the study of message attractiveness. They assert that humans are more likely to store and remember "vivid" rather than pallid information, implying that vivid events and issues are more likely to enter a channel. "Information may be described as vivid, that is, as likely to attract and hold our attention and to excite the imagination, to the extent that it is (a) emotionally interesting, (b) concrete and imagery-provoking, and (c) proximate in a sensory, temporal, or spatial way" (Nisbett & Ross, 1980, p. 45). Therefore, a story about a homeless family's efforts to celebrate Christmas for its 4-year-old child should be more likely to enter a channel (and to pass by individual gates) than a dry, statistical accounting of the plight of the homeless during the holidays. If the story can be made more image provoking—the little girl with long, dark hair who has always wanted a doll who looks just like her—then its chances are even better. If the girl and her family are seen by the source "living" in a local park, then the story is still more likely to get into the channel.

Stories about people we know are more interesting to us than those about people we do not know. Stories about people for whom we have strong feelings are more interesting than those on people about whom we are neutral. Concrete details about individual people, their actions, or their situations make the information more "imaginable," thus prompting the production of cognitive images. Information obtained firsthand is more vivid than that obtained secondhand. Anecdotes and case histories may be more likely to enter a channel than data summaries (Nisbett & Ross, 1980).

Vivid information is more likely to be remembered because concreteness and imaginability promote both recognition and recall. Possibly for this reason, pictures—which are concrete and both provide and elicit images, whether in print or on television—are remembered better than verbalizations (Nisbett & Ross, 1980, p. 51). Vivid information may also recruit from memory schemas that suggest whether it is appropriate for an information unit to enter a channel (p. 54).

Items of high quality or attractiveness should be more likely to pass the gate. Items that duplicate those that have already passed a gate are less likely to get through. Items of doubtful truthfulness should be less likely to pass the gate—at least in the form received; a process of second-guessing (Hewes & Graham, 1989) may result in the message being reinterpreted. In addition, items that attack the gatekeeper's beliefs are thought to cause cognitive stress, and this may either slow the decision process or cause errors in judgment, such as whether to categorize a message as hard or soft news (Greenberg & Tannenbaum, 1962).

The forces in front of and behind gates. As discussed earlier, one of Lewin's (1951) central ideas was that there are "forces" in front of and behind each gate and that the forces tend to change polarity (change from positive to negative and vice versa) as an item passes through the gate. For example, a news story may be difficult to cover if it occurs far away in a location where a television network has few journalists. This negative force (remote location) would tend to work against the passage of the story into the first news gate. If, however, network executives deem that the story is important enough to devote large resources in getting people and equipment to the remote location to cover it—in other words, to passing the story through the gate—then the previously negative force becomes positive: Cost becomes value. Because the network has spent so much money getting coverage of the story, it will be more likely to ensure that the story passes through subsequent gates and is given prominent play on the evening news.

In another example, consider what Gandy (1982) calls "information subsidies." These are messages prepared outside the mass media—for example, by a public relations firm—in a format that the media can easily use. The subsidized message may be attractive to the television network (a positive force) if it is of high quality and requires little or none of the network's resources to use. Therefore, we expect that it would tend to pass by the first gate. Once in the news organization, however, the positive force might turn negative: "This comes from a PR firm; should we use it? Can we trust it?"

The issue of forces is far from fully elaborated, however. There are at least four issues involving forces that Lewin (1951) did not address. The first is that forces may retain their polarity (e.g., remain positive) after passing through a gate. Do positive and negative forces always have to change polarity on the other side of a gate? Not necessarily. For example, the more newsworthy an event is (positive force), the more likely it is to pass through the first news gate. Once inside the organization, its newsworthiness will not hinder its passage through subsequent gates by becoming a negative force; newsworthiness should facilitate movement through subsequent gates—at least until it becomes "old" news. The point is that the polarity of forces before and behind the gate is not constant, but there is no general rule governing direction and no guarantee that change will occur.

The second issue is that forces may vary in strength, some conflicting with others. Strong forces should, by definition, have more of an effect on the movement of items past gates and through channels than weak forces. For example, Nisbett and Ross (1980) suggest that vivid items (i.e., those that are striking or lifelike) generate more extreme attitudes than pallid items, perhaps because they remain in thought longer. The force strength of a news item should be positively related to how vivid the message is: A vivid message (such as an account of a murder) should exert a stronger positive force than a pallid message (such as murder rate statistics). Therefore, we might expect not only that vivid items will generate stronger forces than pallid items but that the force will be positive and thus will facilitate movement of the item through the channel and past the gate. Why? Because vivid items get more attention and interest than pallid ones, and the fact that they tend to be thought about more may reflexively cause the gatekeeper to conclude that a vivid item is more important: "If it weren't important, why would I be thinking about it so much?" (Nisbett & Ross, 1980).

A third issue is that forces may have a bidirectional influence through a gate, with forces behind a gate influencing those before the gate. The number of items in front of or behind the gate may affect how strong the forces are that act on them. For example, if in front of the gate there are three stories about one event and only one story about another, this may increase the collective strength of the three-item event and improve the likelihood that one of the three stories will be selected to pass the gate. Conversely, if three stories about an event have already passed through the gate, this may weaken the strength of the force acting on a fourth story that is still in front of the gate. If these suppositions are true—and there is support for them in White's (1950) original study—then passage of items through gates may not simply be unidirectional with the forces in front of the gate affecting those behind it but not vice versa. This raises the question of the circumstances under which forces behind a gate affect the forces in front of it. There is, however, no theoretical principle to address this point.

Fourth, we should consider how differing forces and polarities affect the entire gatekeeping process, not just selection. As indicated in an earlier section, Donohue, Tichenor, and Olien (1972, p. 43) define gatekeeping as also including the shaping, display, timing, withholding, or repetition of messages. By conceptualizing gatekeeping as a broader process—not simply selection—Donohue et al. go beyond Lewin's (1951) theory, and we can readily see how the forces around a gate influence these broader gatekeeping processes. Not only should items with a positive force be more likely to be selected (pass the gate), they should also be shaped in an attractive or attention-getting fashion, get more coverage, be timed to attract the largest audiences, and be repeated. Items with negative forces would be less likely to be selected; although some negative items may be selected, many will be purposely withheld or censored. If messages with negative forces are selected, then they will be given unfavorable shaping, display, timing, and will be unlikely to be repeated. Thus the nature of the forces—their number, strength, and polarity—helps determine what happens to a message once it enters a communication organization.

Individuals' personal attitudes and values. What kinds of attitudes and values do people bring with them to the gate? How do these affect gatekeeping decisions? For example, White (1950) said that Mr. Gates's personal attitudes and values had a strong influence on his selection of news items. This is supported by Flegel and Chaffee's 1971 study of reporters at two newspapers, one liberal and the other conservative. The authors departed from traditional gatekeeping studies by asking reporters directly how much they were influenced by their own opinions and by those of editors, readers, and advertisers. Reporters on both papers indicated that they were most strongly influenced by their own opinions, followed by editors', readers', and advertisers' opinions:

Thus we may say that they ignored external social pressures, including those within their own occupational bureaucracies, but did not ignore their own personal convictions—that this process was apparently a very conscious one. . . . A professional reporter should recognize his prejudices so that he can take them into account in striving for an objective report. Objectivity is no less a goal in reporting because it is not invariably achieved. (Flegel & Chaffee, 1971, pp. 650-651)

The gatekeeper's personal opinion may also influence the selection of arguments in news stories and editorials. In an experiment where students were asked to write editorials in accord with company editorial policy, those whose opinions were originally against the policy wrote the most one-sided editorials. Those who agreed with policy were more likely to bring in both sides of the argument. In the same study, students who were asked to write news stories that conflicted with their own attitudes used fewer facts that supported their own viewpoint than did those whose attitudes were consistent with the story (Kerrick, Anderson, & Swales, 1964).

When one of Jack Anderson's 1980 "Washington Merry-Go-Round" columns told of a secret plan for the United States to invade Iran, some newspapers did not publish it. Whereas public concern centered on whether such a publication would endanger national security, editors' decisions about whether to publish the column centered on their assessments of Anderson's credibility and their feelings about the need to provide readers with important information (Anderson, 1982). Judd (1961), however, shows substantial variance in journalists' predispositions and personalities and suggests that some gatekeepers are passive, merely conforming to images of what they think readers want or to ideas about objectivity. Differing reportorial styles and interpretations of what management wants may result in differing gatekeeping decisions.

Reanalyses of the Mr. Gates study by McCombs and Shaw (1976) and Hirsch (1977) suggest that the gatekeeper's personal attitudes may not be as important as White (1950) suggested. These studies show that the categories of news that Mr. Gates selected mirrored what was provided to him by the wire services. Therefore, McCombs, Shaw, and Hirsch concluded that the wire services' budget of news items in various categories is a far more important determinant of Mr. Gates's selections than his personal opinions. We will pursue this idea further in a later section on the organizational level of analysis. The literature on boundary roles suggests that the observed correlation between wire service content and Mr. Gates's choices may *not* be due to Mr. Gates following the lead of the wires.

Social Roles of Gatekeeping

This section will explore gatekeeping's role in the larger society. How do gatekeepers come up with the view of social reality that they transmit to others? What role does gatekeeping play in the creation of the audiences' perceived social reality? Does gatekeeping result in a condensed version of an objective reality or does it mold social reality?

The role of gatekeepers in creating the media's picture of social reality. The process of gatekeeping is the process of creating social reality: If an event is rejected by the media I use, it probably will not become part of the social reality I perceive. If the event is accepted and displayed prominently, then it may not only become part of my version of social reality but it may strongly influence my view of the world. In this section, we look at cognitive processes that cause the communication worker to present a certain view of social reality.

We know that two witnesses to an event may not give identical accounts of the action, and many studies show instances in which the media version of reality does not perfectly match a measure of reality from another source. Lang and Lang (1953), for example, showed that the televised version of a parade differed in important ways from the view of observers stationed along the parade route. Merely covering an event requires that selection take place, and the rules of selection (i.e., based on conceptions of newsworthiness) may result in a version of reality that is more interesting and that seems more important than the event itself. The press, after all, sells news reports, not the events themselves. There is a general tendency to make their product as attractive as possible.

Those gatekeepers who see their job as the neutral transmission of an objective reality to the audience (Johnstone, Slawski, & Bowman, 1972) may try to select items that, on the whole, provide a representative picture of the day's events. As Nisbett and Ross (1980) point out, however, application of the *representativeness heuristic*—an automatic and nonreflective "goodness of fit" comparison of one item with others in a category—can result in inference errors. For example, a news gatekeeper automatically assesses how newsworthy a message is by unconsciously comparing its features with those of messages that are known to be in the category "news."

Unfortunately, the representativeness heuristic can lead to a nonrepresentative selection of items, especially if the items are in the "social domain" (such as news) instead of in the "physical domain" (Nisbett & Ross, 1980). For example, it may be easier for a botanist to correctly classify an oak tree on the basis of limited information than it would be for a journalist to say whether an event is newsworthy based on a similarly limited amount of information. For items in the social domain, the decision is more complex, requiring more information to identify the correct category. The result is that an automatic—I know news when I see it—classification may not result in a representative picture of the world (see also Kahneman et al., 1982).

Another source of potential error in a gatekeeper's presentation of the day's events is the group dynamics of media workers, particularly their level of social cohesiveness. Irving Janis (1983, p. 9) coined the term *groupthink* to

refer to a mode of thinking that people engage in when they are deeply involved in a cohesive ingroup, when the members' strivings for unanimity override their motivation to realistically appraise alternative courses of action. . . . Groupthink refers to a deterioration of mental efficiency, reality testing, and moral judgment that results from ingroup pressures.

Janis's (1983, p. 13) central proposition is this: "The more amiability and esprit de corps among the members of a policy-making in-group, the greater is the danger that independent critical thinking will be replaced by groupthink, which is likely to result in irrational and dehumanizing actions directed against out-groups."

Are gatekeepers subject to the groupthink phenomenon? Janis (1983, pp. 174-175) divides symptoms of groupthink into three categories. First, group members may overestimate their group's power and morality. Journalists may feel that they are invulnerable, causing them to take more risks than one ordinarily would. Some journalists consider themselves protected from lawsuits by the First Amendment, whereas others may believe that they are exempt from physical harm. (More than 40 Western journalists were captured by Iraqi troops during the 1991 war in the Persian Gulf; chafing under U.S. control of reporters, they had set off on their own into the war zone.) Journalists may also assume that their actions are inherently moral, and, therefore, they do not question the ethical consequences of their actions. The public's "right to know" can be a defense against journalists' violations of ethics and provide a moral base from which to give people everything the journalists think they need to be responsible citizens.

Janis's second set of groupthink symptoms involves closed-mindedness. Journalists may ignore information that counters their proposed actions and conceive of all their critics as evil, weak, or stupid. To the extent that journalists consider themselves the correct arbitrators of what the public needs to know, they will be closed to alternative points of view.

The third set of symptoms involves pressures on the group's members toward uniformity. Each member of the group self-censors doubts about the group's actions, and a majority decision is accepted as representing unanimity. If a member dissents, direct pressure for conformity is applied by other members. Some members of the group take on the role of "mindguards"—those who protect the group from contrary information. Pressures toward uniformity may be especially prevalent among communication workers. Journalists socialize with other journalists (Johnstone et al., 1972) and tend not to be personally involved with nonmedia organizations. Editorial meetings decide the newspaper's editorial policy on issues, and journalists have a strong tendency toward "pack journalism," with news gatekeepers validating their own selections by observing what other gatekeepers do. In Crouse's (1972) study of how reporters covered a presidential campaign, he observed that the "boys on the bus," as he called them, knew that their stories would be questioned if they deviated too far from what other reporters had said. Journalists have an ever-present need to validate their own news sense. According to Bernard Cohen (1963, p. 83):

> Foreign affairs correspondents go hand in hand in quest of news, looking everywhere together, yet each one also looking on his own and hoping that his narrow channel of the broad front will yield a different, or an original, or the first, discovery. . . . Yet he is never so free of the need to validate his news sense that he can fail to keep a close eye on the prevailing market for news, like a general guarding his flanks.

On the other hand, gatekeepers may not be subject to the groupthink phenomenon if any of three antecedent conditions is absent (Janis, 1983, pp. 176-177). First, the group must be insulated, with few sources of alternative information or evaluation. Second, group leaders must use their power and prestige to influence others in the group. Third, there must not be any norms about how to make decisions. Some gatekeepers are isolated and others are not. Do these conditions apply to gatekeepers? To the extent that a gatekeeper does not bring in outside information (or relies on a restricted group of sources, such as government officials), he or she will be more isolated and, therefore, more susceptible to groupthink. Most communication organizations are hierarchically organized, with people in managerial positions imposing their decisions on those beneath them. However, many norms exist to guide gatekeepers on how to handle messages (see the section on communication routines). This suggests that the groupthink analysis may only apply to communication gatekeepers in situations where no routines exist to guide decision making. Tuchman (1974) suggests that journalists are not able to anticipate every potential event and message, although most newsroom procedures are designed to "routinize the unexpected." It is in these unexpected situations that journalists may be most subject to groupthink and provide a view of reality based on incorrect assumptions.

Effects of the gatekeepers' version of social reality on the audience. The most obvious effect of gatekeeping on the audience is cognitive—shaping the cognitions of the audience as to what the world is like—what some have called "cognitive maps" (Ranney,

1983). Information that gets through all the gates becomes part of social reality, whereas information that stops at a gate does not. But news decisions also include an evaluative dimension and have the potential to influence attitudes and opinions (Alexander, 1981). For example, as agenda-setting research points out (McCombs & Shaw, 1976), issues that get through the gates most often are accorded the most importance by the audience and affect public opinion on that issue. But we also need to recognize that the gatekeeping process can affect audience attitudes and opinions directly to the extent that supporting or conflicting messages pass through the gates. For example, the U.S. military's ability to control access to information about the 1991 Persian Gulf war did not reduce the huge volume of news stories about U.S. involvement in the war, but very few of them were negative. Not only was the war at the top of the news and public agendas, but President George Bush's approval rating reached unprecedented levels in opinion polls following the conclusion of the war.

Media influence on public opinion will be limited, however, by the extent to which media versions of social reality agree. As Noelle-Neumann (1980) points out, the media are most influential in affecting public opinion when they present a consonant version of social reality. Consonance means that the audience has a limited range of information from which to form opinions. We know from research, however, that media depictions of the world are not always consonant; the vast number of decisions made by gatekeepers do not necessarily result in similar images of social reality. In Luttbeg's (1983a) content analysis of more than 100 newspapers in the early 1980s, front pages were found to be dissimilar. The author suggests that such differences—which might be the result either of gatekeeping or of a random process forced by the large number of stories that must be dealt with in a single day—result in views of the world that vary significantly from city to city. Miller, Goldenberg, and Erbring (1979) found differences among cities in public confidence in government, depending on the number of critical news stories that appeared in local newspapers. Network television news seems to vary less. Bantz (1990a) suggests that media organizations (such as ABC, NBC, and CBS) often produce very similar views of the world because they operate within the same news environment, are all influenced by what other media do (see the section on the extramedia and social/institutional level below), and have a tendency to replicate what they've done before.

Those issues or events that are not covered do not exist for most audience members. The existence of a large publicity industry in the United States is based on an assumption that media coverage gives prestige, power, and opportunities to those people and organizations that find their way into the media. The mass media provide a conduit through which groups can reach the larger public. For new ideas, getting media exposure is a contingent condition for acceptance, and groups fight for access to the media and, therefore, to the audience. Whereas media coverage does not ensure acceptance of new ideas—particularly if the ideas are deviant and, therefore, treated as not legitimate (Shoemaker, 1984)—a lack of coverage almost certainly dooms them to failure.

3. Theorizing About Gatekeeping

An important issue in theory building is the *level of analysis* on which the theory is based—in other words, the level of complexity of the social unit being studied. Levels of analysis range from the individual to macroscopic levels such as the nation. In this book, we will apply five levels of analysis to the study of gatekeeping: the individual communication worker (e.g., attitudes), the routines or practices of communication work (such as deadlines or the inverted pyramid), the organizational level (looking at variables such as ownership patterns), the social and institutional level of analysis (including the mass media, advertising, and interest groups), and the social system level (looking at variables such as ideology and culture; Shoemaker with Mayfield, 1987; Shoemaker & Reese, 1991).

Lewin's choice of the terms *gatekeeping* and *gatekeeper* leads one naturally to think about gatekeeping as a process that operates on the individual level of analysis—an individual opens and closes the gates. However, Lewin (1943, p. 64) also suggested that both cultural and psychological variables (recall the "food ideology" of the gatekeeper) would be important in determining people's fare. Schramm (1963, p. 17) urged that gatekeeping be studied in a variety of ways—"the flow of the news through the organization, the points at which decisions are made, the pattern of authority and influence, the kind of values and standards that come into use in given places and under given conditions." These include at least three levels of analysis: Values and patterns of authority and influence are studied at the individual level, decision points and standards are studied at the routines level, and the flow of news through the organization is studied at the organizational level.

Gieber (1964) criticized gatekeeper studies that use the individual level of analysis, suggesting that gatekeeping decisions are influenced not only by the gatekeeper's values but also by newsroom and audience values (the routines and social/institutional levels). In a 1965 study of newspapers' use of wire copy, Gold and Simmons speculated about influences on two levels of analysis, saying that the similar treatment that 24 Iowa newspapers and the Associated Press (AP) gave to various topics could have been due either to similarities in news judgments by the journalists involved (individual level) or to the newspapers' routine of letting the wire service guide their own patterns of emphasis (routines level).

The choice of level leads one to ask some questions and to ignore others. White's (1950) study of Mr. Gates was on the individual level of analysis. This led White to look only at this individual's decisions—why he chose to include some news items and exclude others. But it is obvious that Mr. Gates also acted on behalf of his organization and profession (routines level) and that his decisions were at least partially the result of his role rather than his individual characteristics. Gatekeeping could be studied as solely an organizational-level process, although events have multiple causes, and it is important to separately identify aspects of gatekeeping relevant to each level of analysis.

Individual Level

To what extent are individual communicators responsible for gatekeeping selections? This may vary according to the type of communication organization being studied: Abbott and Brassfield (1989) found that individual television gatekeepers seem to have more decision-making autonomy than their newspaper counterparts. As Tunstall (1971, p. 23) puts it, "There will always be much room for the exercise of discretion by journalists. Even though news may not be what journalists alone make it, journalists constitute one of the important categories of people who make news." When studying individual gatekeepers, we need to look at theories of thinking, that is, how gatekeepers evaluate and interpret messages; theories of decision making; and characteristics of the individual gatekeeper's personality, background, values, role conceptions, and experiences.

Models of thinking. Before a gatekeeper can decide whether a news item should pass through a gate, the gatekeeper must think about the item, considering both its individual characteristics and the environment in which the item resides. Snodgrass, Levy-Berger, and Hayden (1985) outline three theories about the mechanisms of thought: associationism, gestaltism, and information processing.

Associationism is the oldest of the three approaches, essentially representing the stimulus-response school of behavioral psychology. Thought processes are conceived as linear, with one idea recalling related ideas or connecting with other ideas, either remembered or imagined. A stimulus item in the person's environment evokes an associated mental response. Applying this model of thinking to gatekeeping leads us to see gatekeeping as a series of linked associations between an item and others like it: "This news item reminds me of past news items that we have accepted, so it should probably be accepted too"; or "this item is like many others I've already selected today, so I may not need it." As in general stimulus-response models, if an association is positively reinforced, it will be strengthened; negative reinforcements weaken associations. Thus associations change through a process of trial and error. Because stimulus items are routinely categorized, when one element of a category is reinforced, all associated elements are also reinforced. To the extent that gatekeepers use categories to evaluate whether new messages ought to be accepted or rejected, the associative approach can exert a powerful influence. A weakness of the associative approach, however, is that it offers little explanation for innovative thinking such as leaps of intuition—the "hunch" that a big story is about to break.

Gestalt theory conceives of the thinking process holistically, proposing that it is not merely the sum of individual thinking activities. Attention is paid to the structure of the entire process rather than to specific activities. Two types of structures have been identified: reproductive thinking, which taps old information and applies it, and productive thinking, which includes imagination and new uses of information. Unlike associative thinking's chain of associations, gestalt thinking involves continuous thoughts. Success is the result of insight into the demands of the complete task. Relating gestalt theory to gatekeeping, some gatekeepers may conceive of their task as selecting a worldview to be presented to the audience rather than as making a series of in/out decisions. The frame of reference would be a decision about the whole rather than about individual parts: What overall impression have I given about the war so far? What element is missing? What would help people understand what's really happening? The gestalt approach underlies Lewin's (1933) work in Field Theory, which emphasized the dynamic connections between the person and the environment. A strong gestalt approach was not favored by Lewin, however, because the parts would totally lose their independence and exist only in relationship to the whole. Some leeway needs to be given for individually oriented decision making.

The information processing approach conceives of problem solving as a series of logical steps, with a linearity similar to associationism but lacking the assumption of reinforcement. This approach tries to reduce tasks to the minimum cognitive processing functions necessary, such as computer simulations of human thinking. Another dimension of the information processing approach is the study of *channel capacity*, looking at how many unrelated items humans can deal with in short-term memory. When items can be grouped into meaningful chunks, many more items can be processed. This is consistent with Tuchman's (1974) suggestion that journalists group news items into categories as a way of coping with an essentially unmanageable task—selecting from among the vast number of potential news items the relative few that actually make it past all gates. The information processing approach also indicates that an overload of items to process will degrade the quality of that processing, suggesting that gatekeeping decisions made from among many news items may differ from those made on slower news days.

Second-guessing. A theoretical approach to explain how people evaluate and interpret messages has been proposed by Hewes and Graham (1989); they call this process *second-guessing.* It is a cognitive process through which a person tries to "correct" or "debias" a message by bringing in prior knowledge to reinterpret the manifest message.

Figure 3.1 presents Hewes and Graham's (1989) model of the second-guessing process. It consists of four general phases, the first of which is *vigilance.* Vigilance begins at the top of the diagram with the term *message/context.* In this phase, the gatekeeper receives a message from a source and initially interprets it at face value. Because of conflicts with information already in memory or because of cues extracted from the message, some doubt may be brought to bear on the message's truthfulness. If the doubt is low, the message may then be accepted at face value and the process stops. If doubt is high but there is little need for accuracy, then the process would stop with the rejection of the initial interpretation. If, however, the level of doubt is significant and the gatekeeper's need for accuracy is high, then the gatekeeper would proceed to the second stage in the model—*reinterpretation.* It is in this second stage that second-guessing occurs. Because the gatekeeper has significant doubts about the veracity of the message, he or she provides one or more interpretations of the message that are thought to be more accurate than the message taken at face value. The more important it is that information be accurate, the more effort will be expended in coming up with more plausible alternative interpretations. In the *reinterpretation assessment* phase, the gatekeeper evaluates and selects one or more strategies for reinterpreting the message. If the "best" reinterpretation is found, then the gatekeeper may cease analyzing the message. If, on the other hand, the gatekeeper is dissatisfied with the reinterpretations, he or she may continue second-guessing. At some point, the gatekeeper may enter the fourth phase,

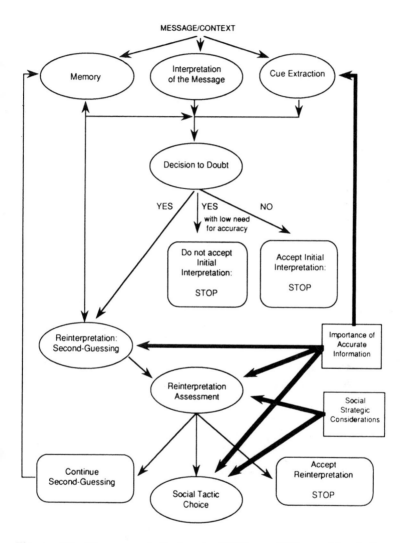

Figure 3.1. Hewes and Graham's (1989, p. 221) model of the second-guessing process. Used by permission.

NOTE: Ellipses represent cognitive processes, standard rectangles represent causal variables, and rounded rectangles represent exit points. Thin arrows carry the results of a cognitive process to the next stage, whereas wide arrows show the causal effects of a variable on a cognitive process.

social tactic choice, in which additional information may be sought to verify or refute various interpretations.

This theoretical approach is important for gatekeeping because it conceptualizes the gatekeeper as an active information processor and provides some understanding of the cognitive process through which gatekeepers decide to allow some messages to pass the gate and to reject others. In addition, to the extent that the gatekeeper's interpretation of the message is incorrect, inferences and actions based on that interpretation will be flawed.

Cognitive heuristics. Gatekeepers are only human, and they experience the same types of cognitive processing as other people. Kahneman et al. (1982) have identified judgmental heuristics, or rules of thumb, that people use in solving problems and making decisions. These cognitive strategies differ from deliberate application of decision rules in that they are generally and automatically applied without conscious consideration. They "are relatively primitive and simple judgmental strategies. . . . The use of such simple tools may be an inevitable feature of the cognitive apparatus of any organism that must make as many judgments, inferences, and decisions as humans have to do" (Nisbett & Ross, 1980, p. 18).

Two of these judgmental strategies include the *availability heuristic* and the *representativeness heuristic* (Nisbett & Ross, 1980). The availability heuristic comes into play when people are asked to judge the frequency of objects or the likelihood of events: Items that are cognitively available (i.e., more accessible from memory or more easily imagined) are likely to be judged as more frequent or likely. The representativeness heuristic helps people decide the category to which an event belongs: The more similar an event's characteristics are to those in the category, the more likely the event is to be placed in the category.

Such judgments are important because they affect behaviors (Nisbett & Ross, 1980). Although Nisbett and Ross did not study gatekeepers, we assume that the same cognitive processes that humans generally go through also apply to gatekeeping. Thus gatekeepers' cognitive judgments of a message will affect their decisions about whether to allow the message to pass through the gate. The availability heuristic makes more cognitively available messages (e.g., those that are more easily remembered) seem more frequent, thus potentially leading the gatekeeper to allow more of them to pass through the gates. The representativeness heuristic helps gatekeepers categorize messages in a variety of ways but into at least two important categories: messages we generally use versus messages we do not. This approach acknowledges the active role of gatekeepers: They do not passively receive messages. Rather, they interpret the messages, resolve ambiguities, make educated guesses about things that they have not observed directly, and form inferences about relationships.

As Nisbett and Ross (1980, p. 28) point out, however, when humans (not just gatekeepers) experience "the rapid flow of continuing social events," their understanding "may depend less on such judgmental procedures than on a rich store of general knowledge of objects, people, events, and their characteristic relationships." Such knowledge structures are sometimes referred to as frames, scripts, prototypes, or schemas. Relevant to the gatekeeping concept, we may ask if, for example, news gatekeepers use a "news schema" to evaluate whether a message qualifies as news (and passes the gate) or does not qualify as news. The nature of the gatekeeper's schema(s) may explain why some messages are allowed to pass the gate and others are rejected: A message may pass because it becomes associated with a news schema, or, conversely, one may be rejected because it is associated with nonnews. The point is that gatekeepers almost never react to messages as unique or original; rather, messages are "assimilated into preexisting structures in the mind" of the gatekeeper (Nisbett & Ross, 1980, p. 36).

Decision making. In contrast with judgmental heuristics, decision-making theories imply the conscious application of rules. Gandy (1982) shows how decision-making theories can be used to study the selection of news items for transmission. From the point of view of the individual, the gatekeeping process is essentially a series of binary decisions—does the item pass through the gate or not? Decisions are "the rational choice between options, based on the expected value to be derived from the pursuit of one option rather than another" (Gandy, 1982, p. 21). Wright and Barbour (1976, p. 58) say that there are four steps in making a decision: problem recognition, defining the pool of alternatives, reviewing relevant information, and applying a decision rule.

Although Wright and Barbour look at decision making from the point of view of an external agent who wishes to influence a consumer decision, rather than from that of the decision maker, their analysis of the general decision process can still be helpful in understanding gatekeeping. Gatekeeping is similar to the consumer decision-making process because gatekeepers may be consumers, producers, and distributors of messages. They "buy" some messages and reject others; also, some of the bought messages will later be "sold" (literally, in the case of the wire services). We will come back to Wright and Barbour's model in the section on how public relations can influence media content.

An editor, for example, may become aware of an environmental problem in his or her local community. Once the problem has been recognized, the editor may conduct an information search to identify the dimensions on which environmental problems might be evaluated, such as in terms of aesthetics, economics, or health. At this stage, interested parties have the opportunity to create messages that will influence the relative importance of such dimensions. The editor may assign reporters to cover various aspects of the overall story; use messages that are available from another source, such as a wire service; or follow up on leads from sources, including public relations-initiated contacts.

Outside influence also is likely at the second stage—definition of alternatives—where sources may constrain the range of information that is available or may emphasize some messages at the expense of others. As Wright and Barbour (1976) point out, if a source can control the range of messages available to a communication organization, then the individual communication worker's decision will be influenced. Making some options more attractive than others is a way of increasing the likelihood that they will pass through the gate, consistent with what Lewin (1947) predicted concerning the role that positive forces play in facilitating the passage of an item through a gate.

At the third stage, the gatekeeper reviews all that he or she knows about the messages that are available for selection. Aspects of the decision process may include the gatekeeper's global impression of the utility or value of the message (Fishbein & Azjen, 1981), an assessment of the probability that the message will meet appropriate criteria, or even a relative evaluation of the criteria themselves. To return to the environmental example, the editor may have similar messages from a wire service, from a reporter, and from a public relations agency. If the editor globally questions the validity of public relations messages, then that option may be closed. Of the remaining two messages, the editor may feel that the wire service story is more likely to meet acceptable standards of newsworthiness (because the wire service has a long record of providing quality stories) but still reject it because the editor gives more value to the innovativeness of the local reporter's story. Messages that are linked with valued attributes are most likely to enter the gate.

At the final stage, the editor must apply a decision rule to determine which aspects of the environmental problem will be covered. The rule chosen will determine which information collected thus far will be most influential in the ultimate decision, and it is likely that different decision rules will be applied in different types of decisions.

Such an extremely rational approach to decision making may not always apply to gatekeeping. In White's (1950) study, Mr. Gates's decisions were deemed by White to be "highly subjective" and involve the gatekeeper's own personal preferences. Mr. Gates's comments often seemed to represent a spur-of-the-moment decision rather than the linear and logical conscious process described above.

In gatekeeping, decision rules are established explicitly or implicitly by organizations, so rules are appropriate for analysis at the routines or organizational levels. Because the application of the rules is carried out by individuals, however, decision-making theories are still relevant to the individual level of analysis. Because people do not always execute rules in the same way, individual-level characteristics are important. When the rules are very explicit and exhaustive, variability in their application from one person to another will be slight. In principle, one could supposedly eliminate variability entirely if a computer could make the decision based on a programmed set of rules, thereby removing human error from the process (or at least holding it constant, because all decisions would be made using the same human-created program). Other variables that affect the application of rules may include the extent to which their application is conscious or habitual, the person's ability to consider multiple objectives and decision dimensions at one time, the person's knowledge about how successful similar decisions have been in the past and how certain the person is that the decision will remain valid in the future, the confidence the person has in the information that helped shape the decision, and the extent to which external sources of information are available (Gandy, 1982).

Wright and Barbour (1976) outline several types of strategies through which a decision can be made:

(1) *Affect-referral strategy*. The decision maker relies on rather vague "feelings" about the available options rather than on a comparison of detailed information about them. The decision could be to pick the "best" message, but the gatekeeper might also pick one that seemed "good" or "good enough." For example, the gatekeeper might hold a global evaluation that topic A is more important than topic B or that a certain amount of information on topic C should be included in every newscast.

(2) *Compensatory model*. The decision maker subjectively evaluates the worth of each option on a number of specific, weighted dimensions and then creates from this an additive index of overall value. Positive and negative attributes would neutralize each other. A television news gatekeeper might, for example, use two dimensions to decide which of the day's stories should be the lead: level of newsworthiness and the quality of the accompanying visuals. Although newsworthiness is overall the most important criterion, the lead story must have good visuals. A story of high newsworthiness but with poor visuals would get a moderate score under this decision-making rule and would be unlikely to be chosen as the lead.

(3) *Lexicographic strategy*. The decision maker identifies one or more dimensions on which the decision should be made and compares all pairs of available options on the most important dimension. If no clear choice results, then the next most important dimension is used as the basis for more pairwise comparisons. Using this rule, a television gatekeeper concerned about visuals would compare story A's visuals with those of story B, those of B with C's, and so on.

(4) *Conjunctive model*. The decision maker identifies minimum (and possibly maximum) desired values on each of the relevant dimensions, then evaluates the options according to whether they fall within the acceptable range on each dimension. For example, the television gatekeeper may have a minimum level of newsworthiness in mind; stories that do not meet the minimum are arbitrarily rejected. Some of these minimums and maximums may be fixed (as might be the case in determining how much to pay for information), but for others the standards may be relaxed if not enough messages meet the criteria. The television

gatekeeper on a slow news day may pass messages through the gate that would be rejected on another.

(5) *Risk models.* The decision maker may evaluate risk of losses or failures associated with each option, selecting the one that entails the least risk. For example, a television gatekeeper may be able to select between information from two sources, one with a past record of dependability and the other of questionable trustworthiness. The risk model predicts the selection of the former.

(6) *Satisficing.* The decision maker takes the first item that meets the minimum criteria. In White's original study (1950), Mr. Gates rejected several stories late in the day because he had already selected similar ones. Mr. Gates did not look at the entire array of stories before making his decisions, he often picked the first one that seemed appropriate.

Another possible decision-making rule, not mentioned by Wright and Barbour, is whether to select the first or last item presented—to use either primacy or recency as the guiding rule. The decision maker selects either the first item that meets minimum criteria or the most recent one (i.e., the newest news). Organizational routines will be important in determining whether the first or the most recent message is selected; although there is an unending stream of potential messages for gatekeepers to consider, most gatekeepers operate under fixed deadlines that encourage an efficient decision-making process while they at the same time prize newness. Primacy may be a more viable decision-making option with modern computer equipment that makes changing one's mind about a message less traumatic and expensive. A 1964 experiment with journalism students by Kerrick et al. showed that students remembered the material presented to them first, particularly if it agreed with company policy.

Values. Whereas the previous section looked at decision-making styles that probably vary between communication workers, in this section, we consider cognitions that are held in common among communication workers. Gans (1979a) has suggested that U.S. journalists share a set of enduring social values and that these values guide the production of news. The values represent a kind of progressivism that is not easily classified as either liberal or conservative: ethnocentrism, altruistic democracy, responsible capitalism, small-town pastoralism, individualism, moderatism, social order, and national leadership.

Ethnocentrism describes the tendency of the U.S. mass media to frame and shape news events according to how well they match U.S. practices and values. Government reform in the Union of Soviet Socialist Republics is compared with the American system. The status of women in Saudi Arabia is compared with that of women who served in the U.S. armed forces stationed there during the Persian Gulf war.

Altruistic democracy refers to media expectations that politics and government should operate in the public interest. Because it is deviation from the ideal that forms the raw material from which news is made, these stories are generally negative in tone: ethics violations by politicians, inefficiency in government, financial corruption, nepotism, and racial injustice. The media compare the day-to-day running of the political system with the ideals set forth by classical political theorists and almost inevitably find politics and government wanting.

The value of *responsible capitalism* holds that, while economic growth and fair competition are desirable, business should not pursue excessive profits or exploit customers or workers. Business sections of the print media are full of features on entrepreneurs and successful managers. Businesses that help the poor or jump on the "green" environmental movement are given favorable coverage. Unions are tolerated as a countervailing force to owners, but strikes are not given favorable coverage if they cause inflation or involve violence.

Small-town pastoralism favors both nature (in the battle against developers of urban areas) and smallness per se. Media coverage of big cities emphasizes their problems, including violence, racism, and pollution, and such stories are contrasted with features on the relaxed existence of small-town dwellers. Development is generally framed as a move from the natural to an artificial environment, as was the case in Austin, Texas, when some developers were stymied by the discovery on their property of a bird that is on the U.S. Environmental Protection Agency's endangered species list. The battle was framed by local media as the bird versus the bulldozer.

Individualism favors "self-made" men and women as well as those who have overcome constraints to their success, including poverty and bureaucracy. In the United States, the media look unfavorably on people who rely on others too much, such as those on welfare. The ideal person is self-actualized and self-sufficient, whereas dependent people are seen as being weak and psychologically underdeveloped (Shoemaker & Reese, 1991). Likewise, individual cars are preferred to mass transit, and socialized medicine is looked on with skepticism.

Moderatism discourages excess or extremism in any form. Shoemaker (1984, p. 75) found that, the more deviant a political group is, the less legitimately it is portrayed in the mass media. Deviant groups (such as the Ku Klux Klan, the Nazis, and the Communists) were given negative labels, such as "self-righteous," "vehement," "killers," "a cabal of conspirators," and "a bunch of lunatics." Centrist groups (such as the League of Women Voters, the Sierra Club, and Common Cause) were given neutral or positive labels, such as "the club," "a nonpartisan group," "savvy," "hardworking," "intelligent," and "fair."

Social order discourages public disorder, such as protest marches, and moral disorder, such as drug use. Gans (1979a) says that there are four kinds of disorder stories: natural, technological, social, and moral. Natural disorder includes earthquakes and floods, whereas technological disorder covers accidents caused by technology, such as a defect in a car's steering causing it to crash. Social disorder includes activities that threaten the peace. As an example, Gitlin (1980, p. 7) described how the media marginalized demonstrations by the 1960s group Students for a Democratic Society by placing delegitimizing quotation marks around terms like "peace" march. Moral disorder covers normative violations that do not threaten social order, such as media calling public attention to young adults' novel hairstyles and dress.

National leadership as a value results in stories on moral and competent leaders, generally individuals, who have "made a difference" in some problem situation. Problems with leadership also make the news, as was the case when Ronald Reagan was U.S. president: Story after story questioned whether he understood the issues and whether he was actually making decisions. Any suggestion that the leader is not totally in control of his or her job is taken by the media as a potentially dangerous sign.

Stories that represent violations of these values should be more likely to pass a gate than those that are congruent with the values, hence the perennial complaint that the media only cover "bad" news. In their study of how world events are covered by the *New York Times* and by ABC, CBS, and NBC, Shoemaker and her colleagues showed that deviant events are more likely to be covered and get more prominent coverage than normative events (Shoemaker, Danielian, & Brendlinger, in press; Shoemaker et al., 1987). To the extent that deviant events represent threats to the status quo, the media may function as agents of social control when they publicize the events. Publicity of deviance can set into action a corrective mechanism that punishes or eliminates the deviant actions.

Characteristics of individual gatekeepers. Lewin (1951, pp. 177-178) says that "to understand and influence food habits we have to know in addition to the objective food channels and objective availability, the psychological factors influencing the person who controls the channels." He classifies these factors into two groups: the cognitive structure and motivation. *Cognitive structure* refers to the terms in which people think and speak about something; *motivation* includes values, needs, and obstacles to overcome.

In his 1950 study, White asked Mr. Gates whether he had any prejudices that affected his story selection. Mr. Gates replied:

> I have few prejudices, built-in or otherwise, and there is little I can do about them. I dislike Truman's economics, daylight saving time and warm beer, but I go ahead using stories on them and other matters if I feel there is nothing more important to give space to. I am also prejudiced against a publicity-seeking minority with headquarters in Rome, and I don't help them a lot. As far as preferences are concerned, I go for human interest stories in a big way. My other preferences are for stories well-wrapped up and tailored to suit our needs (or ones slanted to conform to our editorial policies). (White, 1950, p. 390)

Thus Mr. Gates acknowledges that selection is affected both by his personal and professional cognitive structures ("I am also prejudiced against a publicity-seeking minority with headquarters in Rome") and his motivations ("I go for human interest stories in a big way"). White (1950, p. 386) concludes that Mr. Gates's selections are "highly subjective" and "reliant upon value-judgments based on the 'gate keeper's' own set of experiences, attitudes, and expectations."

To the extent that communicators vary in their experiences, interests, and prejudices, we may see different gatekeeping decisions. This effect may be contingent, however, on the extent to which the communicator has power within the organization. The characteristics of communicators with power to influence the final selection of stories to be transmitted, such as the editor or producer, influence gatekeeping decisions more than the characteristics of those with less authority (Shoemaker & Reese, 1991).

Role conceptions. The communicator's ideas about what his or her job entails can also affect gatekeeping choices. Cohen's 1963 book *The Press and Foreign Policy* identified two basic roles for journalists: as the neutral reporter and as the participant. Neutrals see their job as requiring them to provide factual information to the audience, allowing the audience to make up their own minds about what is true and correct. Participants, on the other hand, do not count on truth being naturally revealed but seek out and develop the story, at times acting as public policymakers in their own right. Support for Cohen's idea came from Johnstone et al.'s (1972) survey, which showed that journalists identify with the neutral and participant roles.

Weaver and Wilhoit (1986) defined three categories: adversarial, interpretive, and disseminator. More than 60% of U.S. journalists interviewed felt that an interpretive/investigative role is important, compared with about half who emphasized disseminating information quickly to the widest possible audience. (About a third of journalists favored both roles.) A third group (17% of the sample) embraced an adversarial role, the press acting as a watchdog of government and big business.

Although these studies do not speculate about how role conceptions influence gatekeeping decisions, it is fairly easy to imagine ways in which this might occur. These roles should cause gatekeepers to "see" different things and to evaluate their worth as news differently. Disseminators would probably deal only with those messages that come to their attention as a regular part of their job, whereas investigators would seek out and develop the stories. Adversaries, on the other hand, would emphasize stories about the misdeeds of government and business, probably at the expense of other kinds of items.

Types of jobs. Bass (1969) suggests that journalists should be divided into news gatherers (writers and reporters) and news processors (such as copy editors). Much gatekeeping research has been done on news processors, including the original Mr. Gates study. When a message reaches a news processor, however, someone else (a news gatherer) has already defined it as meeting some standard of newsworthiness. A full understanding of the gatekeeping process must include both roles. The amount of autonomy a journalist has also may influence gatekeeping. In addition, journalists working in remote news bureaus have more influence on what gets into their medium than do those who work in the central office.

Communication Routines Level

As Lewin described the gatekeeping process, movement through a channel from gate to gate is controlled either by a gatekeeper *or* by a set of impartial rules (1951, p. 186), which we refer to as "communication routines." Routines are "patterned, routinized, repeated practices for forms that media workers use to do their jobs" (Shoemaker & Reese, 1991, p. 85). Such routines exist not only for the news gathering, processing, and transmission process within the mass media (e.g., deadlines, inverted pyramid, news beats) but also for interpersonal communication (e.g., some subjects and words are commonly judged as inappropriate for a mixed gender group). Other routines are medium specific: Television gatekeepers are more likely than their newspaper counterparts to reject news items that do not have good visuals (Abbott & Brassfield, 1989). Newspaper wire editors have been found to slow their rate of accepting wire copy before the deadline, probably because they fill up their allocated space early and retain only enough for late spot news (Jones, Troldahl, & Hvistendahl, 1961).

Within communication organizations, routines develop as a way to minimize the organizational risk of being involved in a libel suit and to protect individual communication workers from criticism by their peers. Tuchman (1972) has identified four strategic procedures that journalists routinely follow in order to claim objectivity: giving conflicting evidence ("both" sides of a story), presenting supporting "facts" (anything commonly accepted as true), quoting what other people say or using quotation marks to call the legitimacy of groups or events into question (e.g., "peace" march), and appropriately structuring information into the inverted pyramid format (i.e., hierarchically arranging the story with the most important information first). Gitlin (1980, p. 7) has referred to "patterns of cognition, interpretation, and presentation, of selection, emphasis, and exclusion" as *frames*:

> Frames enable journalists to process large amounts of information quickly and routinely: to recognize it as information, to assign it to cognitive categories, and to package it for efficient relay to audiences. Thus, for organizational reasons alone, frames are unavoidable, and journalism is organized to regulate their production.

Routines are crucial in determining which items are moved through the channel and which are rejected, and the distinction between individual influences and communication routine influences on gatekeeping must be made if we are to evaluate the extent of each separately. Even when an individual appears to be a gatekeeper, we must ask the extent to which the individual is merely carrying out a set of routine procedures. Where routines are more important, we would see uniformity in selection across gatekeepers. Variation across individuals would indicate that characteristics of the individuals are important.

For example, Sasser and Russell's (1972) study of news judgments in a newspaper, two television stations, and two radio stations showed little agreement on story selection, length, and position *except for the most prominent stories*. This suggests that routine guidelines on story selection influenced gatekeepers' decisions for major news but that, for less prominent stories, gatekeepers' individual preferences (or medium differences) were more important. Hirsch (1977) has suggested that the media's selection of *categories* of news items more closely parallel each other than is the case with *individual stories*. In support of this idea, Stempel's 1962 study found high agreement among newspapers as to what categories of news should be published. In a later study, Stempel (1985) again found substantial agreement among three television networks and six newspapers on the "mix" of news stories by category, but he found disagreement about which specific stories should be used. Routines seem to dictate the overall pattern of stories, and individual gatekeepers decide which particular stories will be used within that standard framework.

In its "routine" form, gatekeeping engages norms of selection that have evolved over the history of mass communication. When gatekeepers allow norms—patterns of established behaviors—to guide their selections, they represent their profession or society more than acting as individual decision makers. This does not mean, however, that individual decisions cannot affect the gatekeeping process. As Homans (1950) points out, an individual's "orders" may guide future behavior. That is, today's individual gatekeeping decision may become tomorrow's selection norm.

Communication routines are well established throughout the industry. Bantz, McCorkle, and Baade (1981, p. 385) compared a local television news operation with a "news factory," pointing out that news work is highly standardized, with "nearly identical reporters and photographers [used] to produce a uniform product within a limited period of time." This factory system, the authors suggest, "reduces a newsworker's personal investment both in the segment he or she helps produce and in the entire newscast. This is a consequence of the interchangeability of newsworkers and the newsworkers' lack of control over the final product" (p. 382).

Routines are quite functional in a communication organization because they provide regularity and manageability in a job that is inherently unmanageable—the "task of transmuting the events of the world into news" (Golding, 1981, pp. 64-65). They are also common to all sorts of organizations, because routinization helps control the flow of work. It is for just such a purpose that journalists categorize events into five categories: soft news, hard news, spot news, developing news, and continuing news (Tuchman, 1974).

Even the presence of routine deadlines within a communication organization can affect choices. When a deadline is imminent, gatekeeping will probably be limited to those messages already on hand, but, when more time is available, the organization may follow up news tips and seek out stories that do not routinely come to the organization (Whitney, 1981). In White's (1950) study, Mr. Gates was also affected by his deadline. As the deadline neared, because of limited space he rejected many stories that would otherwise have been selected.

In Gieber's 1956 study of telegraph editors, routines seemed more important than individual influences. Gieber found the editors to be passive, task-oriented communicators, making no evaluation of the incoming copy other than in terms of how it fit production goals, bureaucratic goals, and relations with others in the newsroom:

> The most powerful factor was not the evaluative nature of news but the pressures of getting the copy into the newspaper; the telegraph editor was preoccupied with the mechanical pressures of his work rather than the social meanings and impact of the news. His personal evaluations rarely entered into his selection process; the values of his employer were an accepted part of the newsroom environment. (Gieber, 1964, p. 175)

This contrasts with Flegel and Chaffee's (1971) finding that newspaper reporters said they were influenced more by their own opinions than by those of readers and editors.

Standardized news values are used not only to determine what will pass the gate but also as working rules to guide the choice of which details of a message will be emphasized or omitted. News values are "the criteria of relevance which guide reporters' choice and construction of newsworthy stories" (Chibnall, 1977, p. 13). Golding (1981, pp. 74-75) says that news values are based on assumptions about three sets of criteria:

(1) *The audience.* Is this important to the audience or will it hold their attention? Is it of known interest, will it be understood, enjoyed, registered, perceived as relevant?

(2) *Accessibility—in two senses, prominence and ease of capture. Prominence:* To what extent is the event known to the news organization, how obvious is it, has it made itself apparent? *Ease of capture:* How available to journalists is the event—is it physically accessible, manageable technically, in a form amenable to journalism; is it ready prepared for easy coverage, will it require great resources to obtain?

(3) *Fit.* Is the item consonant with the pragmatics of production routines, is it commensurate with technical and organizational possibilities, is it

homologous with the exigencies and constraints in program making and the limitation of the medium? Does it make sense in terms of what is already known about the subject?

As Grey pointed out in a 1966 study of a supreme court reporter, part of a journalist's decision about what to let in the gate depends on what other journalists are doing and saying. Journalists feel compelled to validate their own news sense by showing that others are interested in the same story.

The role of communication routines in the gatekeeping process was elaborated by Galtung and Ruge (1965). They specified nine characteristics of a news event that determine its chances of passing through the various media gates:

(1) *Time span.* Events that coincide with the time frame of the media are more likely to pass through media gates.

(2) *Intensity of threshold value.* Events are more likely to pass through media gates if they are of great magnitude or if they have recently increased in magnitude.

(3) *Clarity/lack of ambiguity.* Events whose meaning is in doubt are less likely to pass through media gates.

(4) *Cultural proximity or relevance.* The media are most likely to accept news events that have close cultural relevance for the intended audience.

(5) *Consonance.* Events that are congruent with expectations are most likely to pass through media gates.

(6) *Unexpectedness.* Among consonant events, those that are the most unusual are most likely to be selected.

(7) *Continuity.* The passing of an event through media gates once also makes future information about the event more likely to be accepted.

(8) *Composition.* Because gatekeepers look at the day's news in its entirety, some news items are selected merely because they contrast with others.

(9) *Sociocultural values.* Values of both the gatekeepers and their societies can also influence selection, above and beyond the other eight factors.

Another routine is the application of common news values to a message—values that are imparted through the routine socialization of journalists. A glance at several newspapers' renditions of world events will suggest that gatekeepers' definitions of "news" hold much in common. But what are these news values? Although there is now general agreement that newsworthiness is multidimensional, the number and type of news dimensions seem to vary by study. Factor analysis is used to identify groups of stories that are given similar play in the media. Stempel's (1962) analysis of 156 national news stories in 25 newspapers distinguished six factors of newsworthiness: suspense-conflict, public affairs, human interest, timeliness, positive events, and controversy about politics and government. Buckalew (1969) found five dimensions of newsworthiness: normality, significance, proximity, timeliness, and visual availability. (Prominence was not important in his data.) Badii and Ward (1980) found four dimensions: significance, prominence, normality, and reward. Although proximity is often mentioned as an important news criterion, Luttbeg (1983b) found no evidence that proximity influenced news decisions in a study of 75 newspapers.

Organizational Level

Because it is obvious that communication routines are developed by communication organizations, why treat routines and organizational factors as two levels of analysis? We see the routines level as including communication practices that are common across many communication organizations, whereas we reserve the organizational level for those factors on which communication organizations may vary. In addition, we also locate within the organizational level consideration of how groups' decision-making strategies affect gatekeeping choices.

The study of gatekeeping at the organizational level is essential. Although individuals and routine practices generally determine what gets past the gate and how it is presented, organizations hire the gatekeepers and make the rules. The ability to hire and fire is one of the greatest powers of an organization (Stewart & Cantor, 1982), allowing it to shape its future and change its past. From the organization's point of view, a successful gatekeeper is a person who can perfectly represent its interests. If an organization doesn't like the way the gates are operated, it can fire the gatekeeper.

An organization is "a bounded, adaptive, open, social system that exists in an environment, interacts with elements of it, and engages in the transformation of inputs into outputs having effects on its environment and feedback effects on itself" (Adams,

1980, p. 322). As Bantz (1990b, p. 503) points out, organizations are "constituted in communication" and exist not as "activity systems" but as "symbolic realities." As an organization selects items from among the population of items available, it creates its own symbolic environment. For example, if a news editor fails to select an item about a fire, for the purposes of the newspaper (and even perhaps for its readers), the fire fails to become part of the symbolic environment. For the newspaper, it is as if the fire never happened. As such selections are made, the nature of the organization itself evolves, being continuously changed by its communication behaviors.

Filtering and preselection systems. Hirsch (1970) points out that a gatekeeping-type function (he calls it "preselection") is probably necessary for all industries. "There are always more goods available for possible production and marketing than there are actually manufactured, promoted and consumed" (Hirsch, 1970, p. 4). Some organizations use test marketing to decide which products to carry into production, and the test results act as an organizational gatekeeper. For other organizations, however, including the popular music industry, conventional market research procedures are unreliable, and *preselection systems* have been developed as a substitute. Such a system "filters the available products, insuring that only a sample of the available 'universe' is ever brought to the attention of the general public" (p. 5).

Regardless of the industry, the preselection system has clearly differentiated roles and functions (Hirsch, 1970, 1977): The "artist" provides the creative material, which is identified by an "agent," who acts like a talent scout for the "producer," who supplies the capital necessary to get the product under way. The "promoter's" job is to create and manage anticipated demand, while the "gatekeeper" stands between the industry and its consumers, deciding which products will be recommended or publicized to the "public," the ultimate consumer of the product.

The separation of production and distribution in many communication industries, such as motion pictures and popular music, has created a large number of organizational gatekeepers (Hirsch, 1977, p. 32):

Radio station program directors, book review editors, talk show staffs, and other professionals who select the copy and programming for their organizations act as gatekeepers who filter the output of production organizations like record companies, book publishers, and filmmakers. . . . Their inability to control this aspect of the distribution process provides mass media gatekeepers with substantial power over them, and sets up a situation in which periodic scandals over the latter's efforts to buy influence through forms of "payola" should be expected.

Organizations, including the mass media, act as cultural gatekeepers for the larger society (Hirsch, 1981).

Organizational characteristics. The organization's culture also is built by and affects gatekeeping activities. For example, Bantz (1990b) says that an "elite" organization is likely to define its staff in terms of elites and nonelites (e.g., "stars" and "experts"). Such an organizational culture influences individuals to base their decisions more on criteria developed within the organization than on those from outside—hence few reports from other media organizations or press releases would be used. Individuals in elite organizations develop a collective consciousness that results in an organizational interpretation being placed on new information (Weick, 1979).

Hickey's (1966) experiments with small-group communication suggests that an individual's position within the organization affects the influence he or she has in the gatekeeping process. Gatekeepers who are central in an organizational network will have the highest status and may be valued more by the organization. Centrally located gatekeepers (e.g., publishers or station managers) will have more power to develop organizational policies—written or unwritten—that may influence message selection. For example, Donohew (1967, p. 67) showed a high correlation between publisher attitude and newspaper content and concluded that "publisher attitude appeared to hold up as the greatest single 'force' operating within the news channel." The influence of such organizational policy is not uniform, however; communication workers may interpret or perceive policy in very different ways (Gieber, 1960). Organizations that do not have a rigid bureaucratic structure may permit more latitude in individuals' gatekeeping decisions than those that have a clear hierarchy of authority and decision making. In an organization of hierarchically arranged communication workers, lower-level employees try to "second-guess" their superiors' judgments to increase their probability of being successful in getting their messages transmitted (Tuchman, 1972). This is evidence of a gatekeeping process within the organization—some reporters' stories are used more than others.

Hirsch (1981) indicates that some organizations concentrate on the creation and production of information (e.g., a newspaper), whereas others concentrate on distribution (such as a radio station that plays hit music). These two types of organizations together act as "gatekeepers of ideas and symbols. Cultural change and innovations usually develop within the production sector, and are made known and diffused to wider publics by the distributor organizations" (Hirsch, 1981, p. 187).

Organizational size also may play a role; for example, gatekeepers in larger newspapers might be required to apply organizational rules more and depend on their own idiosyncratic logic less than gatekeepers in smaller newspapers. If the newspaper is shorthanded, gatekeeping may take the form of selecting and processing existing messages; if resources are more plentiful, the gatekeeping process may be extended to following up on potential stories, so that a story is "created" and selected all in the same process (Whitney, 1981; see also Gieber, 1960).

Organizational boundary roles. Boundary roles, as Adams (1980) sees them, are composed of the *activities* that take place among individuals in the organization and people in the environment.[1] These activities include "(1) transacting the acquisition of organizational inputs and the disposal of outputs; (2) filtering inputs and outputs; (3) searching for and collecting information; (4) representing the organization to its external environments; and (5) protecting the organization and buffering it from external threat and pressure" (Adams, 1980, p. 328). People who engage in these activities may be termed *boundary role persons*; of them, those persons who engage in filtering inputs and outputs are called *gatekeepers* (p. 340). For example, AP editors filter outputs when they decide which messages to send on to subscribing newspapers. The newspapers' wire editors filter inputs when they decide which of the messages sent to them by the AP will actually be used. A buyer for a department store performs an analogous role, in selecting which clothing fashions to offer customers.

Filtering inputs and outputs—gatekeeping, from the organizational point of view—amounts to a series of transactions between the organization and those external to it. *Inputs* include the population of messages that come to the attention of the communication organization, and *outputs* comprise those that are selected and transmitted. Gatekeeping, therefore, involves two processes. A boundary role person selects and rejects input messages according to criteria established by the organization. Determining what the outputs should be involves a boundary role person selecting and rejecting from among the input messages according to the criteria of those external to the organization. For example, a wire service reporter is offered many potential news stories from various sources. This gatekeeper selects from among these the inputs that will be communicated to the organization, *using criteria established by the organization.* Within the organization, the stories may be manipulated in a variety of ways—edited, rewritten, material added or deleted, emphases added or deleted, and so on. According to this organizational model, a subset of the input stories will be selected for outputting, *using criteria established by those who will receive the messages.* Therefore, the wire service organization's own criteria should determine which stories will be selected for processing and consideration, whereas criteria established by the organization's media clients should determine which stories are later transmitted to the clients.

This approach is very different than that of the routines level. Although several studies have looked at the extent to which wire service and newspaper patterns of selection are similar (e.g., Gieber, 1956; Hirsch, 1977; McCombs & Shaw, 1976; Todd, 1983; Whitney & Becker, 1982), the assumption of studies conducted on the routines level is that causality runs from the wire service to the newspaper, that is, that newspapers adopt whatever pattern of selection the wire service offers. The organizational boundary activities approach, however, suggests that wire services transmit stories in patterns of selection congruent with their perception of what the newspapers wish to receive. In this conception, the wire service pattern of selection becomes the dependent variable.

This organizational model is indirectly supported by Whitney and Becker (1982). They found support for their hypothesis that the distribution of wire service copy across categories serves as a cue for newspaper editors' selections, but there was no evidence that wire and newspaper editors share underlying news values. They concluded that their study "supports the idea that news as routinely transmitted in stock categories is indeed 'uncritically accepted' in newspaper and television newsrooms" (Whitney & Becker, 1982, p. 65). By contrast, the boundary roles perspective would predict such a finding not because newspaper editors are uncritical but because wire service editors know what newspaper editors want. Patterns of selection would be congruent because the wire service is giving the newspaper what the wire service knows it wants. News values would be different, because the wire service editors' own news values only influence inputs to their organization. Outputs to the newspaper are influenced by wire service editors' perceptions of what the newspaper editors want. Using this perspective, it is quite possible that wire service editors' news values can be different than those of newspaper editors and still result in similar patterns of selection.

In a related example, Cutlip (1954) looked at how a technological change in the way the AP transmitted information to newspapers—specifically, the change from all-capital-letter teleprinter wire to teletypesetter—affected the mix of news that several Wisconsin newspapers offered their readers. This technological change was followed by decreases in the proportion of local news and increases in the amount of AP copy run by several of the papers. Although Cutlip suggests that the power to make the change was in the newspaper editors' hands, he does not have an explanation for why a technological change in wire copy transmission should result in a decrease in local news. The boundary role perspective would suggest that the newspapers began using more AP copy because AP suddenly began doing a better job of giving the newspapers what they wanted.

Although the boundary activities approach sees gatekeepers as following someone else's rules—either their own organization's rules or those of an external organization—there is still individual variation in application of the selection criteria, which Adams (1980, p. 338) refers to as "filtering errors." From the organization's point of view, any deviations from established rules for selection are seen as errors in either acceptance or rejection procedures. *False positives* include inputting or outputting messages that should not have been selected, according to the established criteria. This may be most likely on a "slow" news day. As Stempel (1989) has suggested, the fact that government offices are usually closed on the weekend means that less news is generally available and, therefore, more marginally newsworthy stories pass the gates on these days. *False negatives* occur if messages that should have been input or output are instead rejected. For example, an editor may decide not to send someone to cover a press conference on the assumption that it would be unimportant, only to find out later from the competition that something extraordinary happened.

The organization views such deviations from prescribed rules as having two types of costs: "first, costs associated with direct and indirect losses resulting from the errors; second, opportunity costs" (Adams, 1980, p. 338). There is a tendency for boundary role people to make more false negative than false positive errors, and studies show that "information 'gatekeepers' are guilty of omission, exaggeration, and selective bias in the performance of their roles" (p. 340). These errors "may be moderated to some extent by independent external information—provided, of course, it is not processed by the same gatekeepers!" (p. 341).

Organizational socialization. Learning the norms and values of the organization is called organizational socialization, and a number of stages have been suggested (Jablin, 1982, pp. 256-257). First, "prearrival" or anticipatory socialization involves the person forming expectations about what the job will be like. Next, the "encounter" stage covers the person's entry into the organization, the result sometimes being "role shock," a conflict between what was expected and organizational reality. The final stage is "metamorphosis," where the person tries to be accepted as a full member of the organization. The person may take on a new self-image, establish new relationships with people, take on new values, and learn new behaviors.

Some studies, such as Breed's (1955) analysis of "social control in the newsroom," consider how a journalist is socialized to learn the editorial policies of the organization. Journalists learn from observation and experience what is newsworthy (i.e., acceptable to the employer) and how to avoid libel suits and criticism from peers by using what Tuchman (1972) calls the "strategic rituals of objectivity." The journalist's socialization as a media professional gives him or her what Sigal (1973, p. 3) calls "a context of shared values" with other journalists.

As gatekeeping decisions are made, this context of shared values comes into play. Therefore, not only do gatekeepers make decisions based on their personal criteria (individual level of analysis) and on those routines of communication work that pervade their profession (routines level), they also make decisions based on an organizational mind-set that is the result of organizational socialization. Thinking in terms of cognitive heuristics (Kahneman et al., 1982; Nisbett & Ross, 1980), we can see that gatekeepers' judgments are formed not only by their personal experiences but also by their professional and organizational lives.

In some instances, socialization may only be "skin deep"—the employee suppresses dissident values in order to keep the job or perhaps even to work behind the scenes to further a goal. This was apparently the case with A. Kent MacDougall (1988, p. 23), a journalism professor who says that he was a socialist during a decade of employment with the *Wall Street Journal*. He writes, "I made sure to seek out experts whose opinions I knew in advance would support my thesis. . . . Conversely, I sought out mainstream authorities to confer recognition and respectability on radical views I sought to popularize."

Extramedia, Social/Institutional Level

Although we have defined gatekeeping as an activity performed by a communication organization and its representatives, we must recognize that communication organizations exist within a social system alongside other social institutions, many of which affect the gatekeeping process. We will discuss several of these, showing how each may influence both selection and shaping of messages as they approach and pass (or not) through the gates.

Sources. In Westley and MacLean's (1957) model (see Figure 1.3), the media are the channels through which information passes on its way from the source to the audience member. However, as Sigal (1973, p. 120) points out, channels may also be defined as "the paths by which information reaches the reporter." Because in many cases media workers do not themselves experience events, the version of reality as processed by sources is extremely influential in determining what comes to the attention of the media. Not only are the procedures that journalists use to identify and select sources an important part of the gatekeeping process (Chibnall, 1975, 1981), but also the sources' own vested interests will affect what they make available to the media worker. Economically and politically powerful sources have more access to the media and, therefore, more opportunity to insert messages into media channels (Gans, 1979b). Resource-poor groups may have to resort to deviant acts to attract media attention (Goldenberg, 1975).

Sources may either facilitate or constrain the movement of information through channels they control, thus affecting the introduction of an item into the media channel. The extent to which the source's and journalist's frames of reference overlap will determine how formal the communication between the source and journalist is (Gieber & Johnson, 1961). When reporter and source frames of reference are completely separate, communication is more formal than when there is overlap. Sources believe that reporters should be "open" gatekeepers, essentially just passing unmediated information straight through the gate. Reporters, on the other hand, want sources to be "open-door" informants, giving the reporter all the information available and letting the journalist decide whether and how information passes through the gate (Gieber & Johnson, 1961, p. 297).

A coorientational model (Dyer & Nayman, 1977; McLeod & Chaffee, 1973) may be used to study relationships between journalists and sources. Both sources and gatekeepers benefit from their mutual relationship, with the sources getting access to target audiences through the mass media and gatekeepers getting access to someone who can regularly provide credible information. The gatekeeper's need for regular, credible information results in a dependence on bureaucratic sources (Gandy, 1982), but identification with the source may be an important contingent condition for the extent to which the source controls content (Donohue et al., 1972, p. 58). For example, gatekeepers who identify with police are more likely to allow the police to influence what passes through gates. We should not assume, however, that gatekeepers uncritically accept all information provided by sources. Because sources have their own agendas to push, gatekeepers have to actively filter out falsehoods and interpret messages in light of what is known about the source, event, or issue (see "second-guessing"; Hewes & Graham, 1989).

Audiences. Scholars disagree about whether audiences can affect gatekeeping decisions. Gieber (1960, p. 204) says that news selection "has no direct relationship to the wants of readers"—being instead influenced by socialization to the communication organization. Donohew (1967) found that community opinion was unrelated to gatekeeper behaviors. On the other side of the argument, Pool and Shulman (1959, p. 143) show that reference group theory may explain how audiences affect communicators: "The messages sent are in part determined by expectations of audience reactions. The audience, or at least *those audiences about whom the communicator thinks,* thus play more than a passive role in communication." In their study, good news was reported more accurately than bad news, possibly because the transmission of good news is seen as a favor to the audience that will be received with gratitude. Reporters may fear that bad news, on the other hand, will alienate the audience, and the reporter "may therefore distort it, either to soften its edge or because anxiety engendered by having to report it makes him less efficient" (p. 156).

Although Gieber (1963, p. 9) says that "it would be a testament of folly to assume . . . that the newsman knows his readers with any realistic degree of intimacy," he also suggests that "introjective" journalists—those who take on the values and feelings of the audience—will be influenced by their perceptions of what the audience wants. Introjection occurs when the audience's values and feelings are internalized, changing the journalists' cognitive system. On the other hand, the "projective" journalist assumes that the audience's values and feelings are similar to his or her own. Projective gatekeepers will follow their own personal judgments, assuming that the audience will concur. Introjective gatekeepers—probably more rare—will "catch" the concerns of their audiences, and gatekeeping will be more influenced by the gatekeepers' perceptions of what the audience wants than by the gatekeepers' personal values and feelings.

Organizational theories about boundary activities (Adams, 1980) suggest that gatekeepers who perform "output" tasks—those who decide which, from among all the stories available, will be sent to the audience—make selection decisions based on criteria established by those external to the communication organization, including audiences. Therefore, gatekeepers' perceptions about what the audience wants should be important in guiding their decisions. This idea was offered earlier by Westley and MacLean (1957). Media gatekeepers (represented by the letter "C" in Figure 1.3) select messages for transmission that will give the audience what it needs or wants. Why? Because, say Westley and MacLean, a mass medium will survive only to the extent that it serves the audience's needs. There are many media in competition with one another for the audience's attention; the one that best meets the audience's needs will be most successful. The media act as "agents" for the audience, providing the audience with "a more extended environment" (Westley & MacLean, 1957, p. 34). Cohen (1963) found that journalists justify their foreign affairs gatekeeping choices by saying, "We print what we know the public will want to read" (p. 125), even though their ideas of what the public wants vary dramatically.

Markets. In profit-making organizations, the gatekeeping process is part of the overall process of maximizing income and minimizing expenditures. The rules that govern gatekeeping should be shaped to maximize market appeal, and, therefore, gatekeeping rules might vary according to market characteristics. In Donohue, Olien, and Tichenor's (1989) study, weekly newspaper editors in small, homogeneous communities were found to give advertising a higher priority than editors of daily newspapers in large, pluralistic communities. This may occur because small-town editors are responsible for both business and editorial decisions, whereas business decisions in big-city newspapers are more likely to be made by specialists outside the news department. Harmon (1989) showed that local television news gatekeepers admitted to planning sensational, sex-related content for ratings "sweeps" weeks as a way of attracting a larger share of the market to their stations.

Advertisers. For mass media that are supported primarily by commercial sponsorship, advertisers can exert substantial influence on what gets into the channel, what gets selected, and how it is shaped. As Altschull (1984, p. 254) asserts: "The content of the press is directly correlated with the interests of those who finance the press. The press is the piper, and the tune the piper plays is composed by those who pay the piper." Mass media gatekeepers—both entertainment and news—frequently select shows they know will attract both a large audience and advertising dollars. Fink (1989, p. 40) says that some newspapers have cultivated high-income readers by "intentionally structuring our news content primarily for [them]. We also market selectively, concentrating circulation drives in the right neighborhoods—those predicted to yield high demographics." *Vanity Fair* magazine's editor pulled the magazine out of a 1984 economic slump by running stories on fashion designers who were the magazine's major advertisers. The April 1989 issue carried 37 pages of ads from people who had previously been given favorable editorial coverage in the magazine (Lazare, 1989). This is not a new phenomenon: In the early days of radio, whole programs were developed and produced by advertising agencies to provide a showcase for their products. Advertiser control over television "soap operas" remains strong today (Cantor & Pingree, 1983).

Gatekeepers at women's magazines apparently operate under self-imposed constraints against running stories about the health risks of smoking. For example, Kessler (1989) investigated the editorial and advertising content of six major women's magazines (e.g., *Cosmopolitan* and *Good Housekeeping*) to see whether the presence or absence of tobacco advertising would be related to the amount of editorial content about the health hazards of smoking—"the number one cancer killer of women" (Kessler, 1989, p. 319). Although women's health was a major topic in the magazines, there was almost no editorial content about any health hazards of smoking, even in *Good Housekeeping,* which did not accept tobacco advertising. The *GH* health editor told Kessler that plans for a major story on the health hazards of smoking have been "cut down time and time again by people who make the big decisions," because the link between lung cancer and smoking is "not very appealing" and "too controversial" (p. 322). As Kessler pointed out, even though *GH* could not lose tobacco advertising income, it might lose advertising revenue from non-tobacco subsidiaries of the tobacco conglomerates.

Government. In Rivers's (1965, p. 129) analysis of "the news managers" in Washington, D.C., he writes that the "control of information is central to power" to make his point about how the government attempts to control the mass media by managing the flow of information. This is not a new phenomenon. Franklin Roosevelt was so savvy in his understanding of news that Arthur Krock of the *New York Times* said: "He could qualify as the chief of a great copy desk" (cited in Rivers, 1965, p. 134). For all of Harry Truman's being known as honest and open, the size of the Executive Branch's "information" and "editorial" jobs doubled during his presidency. They doubled again during Dwight Eisenhower's first four years in the office, and his chief publicist, James Hagerty, made decisions about what would and would not be released.

Interest groups. An interest group, such as Common Cause, the Sierra Club, or Accuracy in Media, is formed of individuals who want to communicate their position on issues. Three types of interest groups are relevant to gatekeeping: those involved in promoting their issue stance, those attempting to alter media content, and those that do both.

The first type of group (e.g., Mothers Against Drunk Drivers) uses the media to get information out about its programs and issue positions. These groups attempt to influence media gatekeepers not only to include messages about their groups but also to ensure that the messages are favorable. They use public relations as a tool to reach their target audiences through media gatekeepers.

The second type of interest group (e.g., Accuracy in Media) exists for the express purpose of changing media content. These groups criticize the media and/or individual gatekeepers and try to affect the gatekeeping process. These groups can exert a double influence on content: Not only do their criticisms get on the news agenda (thereby replacing messages that would otherwise have been selected by a gatekeeper), but they also may cause revisions of media practices or policies. For example, one organization that specifically targets media gatekeepers is the American Family Association, self-described as "a Christian organization promoting the Biblical ethic of decency in American society with primary emphasis on TV and other media" (*Journal of the American Family Association*, 1989, March, p. 2). AFA members send protest postcards to companies that advertise on television programs that the AFA deems offensive.

The third type of interest group uses the media to promote a position and also occasionally tries to influence the gatekeeping process, sometimes by providing "guidelines" for covering topics of interest to the group. For example, in 1968 the American Bar Association adopted its "fair trial-free press" guidelines: By 1976, 23 states had adopted voluntary press-bar guidelines that specified how the media should cover crime and trials. In their study of compliance with the ABA guidelines, however, Tankard, Middleton, and Rimmer (1979) found that newspapers operating under a voluntary press-bar agreement were no more likely to follow the ABA guidelines than were those that had made no such agreement.

Public relations. All kinds of organizations conduct public relations campaigns, often using the media to focus public attention. To the extent that these campaigns are successful, media content is affected directly (through the publication of press releases) and indirectly (through calling the media's attention to the problem). Informal public relations efforts also help organizations that are not able to afford paid advertising, but, for a major public relations campaign, the cost can rival that of advertising.

One way to get one's message across is by designing and holding events that the news media will cover, such as demonstrations and protests (Wolfsfeld, 1984). Boorstin (1971) has called these "pseudoevents." A pseudoevent occurs only because someone planned or incited it, and its primary purpose is to get media coverage. An example of a pseudoevent is a demonstration planned and executed by a group that opposes the sale of *Playboy* magazine at a local convenience store for the express purpose of getting media attention. The pseudoevent/demonstration lasts only as long as the media remain to cover it. This is in contrast to a spontaneously occurring complaint by a patron of the store against its sale of the magazine. Such a natural event is not timed to coincide with media deadlines, neither is its duration tied to the presence of reporters and cameras. A celebration of the 40th "birthday" of *Playboy* would also be a pseudoevent; nothing has really happened, but there may be valuable publicity in the anniversary announcement itself. Why do the media cover pseudoevents? While a pseudoevent fulfills the interest group's need to get media coverage to reach the public, it also fulfills the media's need for news. Well-managed pseudoevents include good photo opportunities, which make them particularly attractive to television.

Other media. Just as some journalists act as "agenda-setters" for others, some media organizations act as agenda-setters for the rest (Bantz, 1990a). The *New York Times* seems to be especially influential in leading to other media's coverage of a topic, as Reese and Danielian (1989; see also Danielian & Reese, 1989) showed in their study of intermedia agenda-setting on the drug issue. Other influential media include the *Washington Post,* the *Los Angeles Times,* and the *Wall Street Journal* (Bantz, 1990a). These newspapers are read every day by thousands of journalists who are searching for ideas for stories they too might cover. The influence of other media on gatekeeping may be particularly important in situations when other influences may be slight, such as when individual gatekeepers lack strong personal opinions about the topic or no selection norms exist (Cohen, 1963).

To what extent do newspapers depend on wire services for guides as to which topics should be given the most play? In his 1959 study, Stempel found six Michigan dailies' selection of wire service stories agreed only about a third of the time. Todd (1983) also found some agreement between the *New York Times* service and newspapers in news selections, particularly among the top stories. Harmon (1989) found substantial agreement between newspapers and local television news in the same market, suggesting that not only do the gatekeepers all begin from roughly the same set of events but they also pay attention to each other's news decisions.

Social System Level

Gatekeeping has clear ties to the social system: Lewin (1947) first discussed gatekeeping as something that must be understood if one is to institute social change—changes in diet, in his example. Lewin believed that not everyone in a society is equally important in the process of social change; the gatekeeper is the key. Of the many forces that surround the gate, some of the most important operate at the social system level of analysis, forming the basis for other levels of influence. We will discuss several system-level variables: culture, societal interests, societal structure, and ideology.

Culture both influences the kinds of items that are allowed to pass a gate and is influenced by them. Just as, in Lewin's (1951, p. 178) example, some foods are appropriate for some cultures and not others, the value placed on news items may vary across cultures. Although some news items are objectively available, they are not culturally available. For example, at one time in the United States, newspapers did not cover rape and child abuse in the open manner with which the topics are discussed today. In many countries, these topics are still not reported.

Riffe, Ellis, Rogers, Van Ommeren, and Woodman (1986) looked at network television news between 1973 and 1981, finding that the news mix in the three networks is highly correlated. The authors speculate that "the view of the world produced in the networks' news package [is similar to] . . . the kind of events that populate the world" (p. 321). Brown (1979) discusses how gatekeeping may be affected by societal interests: He compared media coverage of population and family planning items with an index of business instability between 1935 and 1964. The results showed that population growth and family planning coverage correlated strongly with business instability. That is, the less stable business institutions were, the more the press published population and family planning stories, possibly because families are hesitant to have more children when the parents' jobs are in jeopardy. Brown (1979, p. 679) concluded:

> Gatekeeping in the area, far from being a random process, faithfully mirrors the perceptions of society. . . . The gatekeeper decisions, while made subjectively, are closely attuned to audience interests and the environment which sparks those interests rather than being largely a product of random pressures of the publication process.

The level of structural pluralism in a social system also has been shown to affect gatekeeper's decisions. In a 1986 study,

Tichenor, Olien, Donohue, and Griswold showed that 78 Minnesota editors' opinions changed over 20 years to reflect the increasing diversity and pluralism of the society. Gatekeepers' priorities shifted to emphasize "a more urbanized, pluralistic social structure" (p. 10).

Gatekeeping also can be affected by the ideology of the social system in which the gatekeepers exist. Raymond Williams (1977, p. 109) defines ideology as "a relatively formal and articulated system of meanings, values and beliefs, of a kind that can be abstracted as a 'world-view' or a 'class outlook.' " On the social system level, ideology becomes not an individual's belief system but an integrated worldview shared by practically everyone in a social system. In the United States, for example, ideology includes a belief in the capitalistic economic system, the Protestant ethic and individualism, and liberal democracy (Shoemaker & Reese, 1991). This ideology is closely mirrored in the themes identified by Gans (1979b) in his study of working definitions of "what's news."

According to Gramsci's (1971) theory of hegemony, the ideological system within which gatekeepers exist causes them to select items that serve the purposes of powerful elites. As Gitlin (1980, p. 253) defines it, hegemony is the "systematic (but not necessarily or even usually deliberate) engineering of mass consent to the established order." This implies that the mass media serve as agents of the powerful, creating a false consciousness for the audience that serves to retain the dominance of powerful elites. The gatekeeping process could be one tool for shaping that consciousness: In a circular argument reminiscent of structural functionalism, gatekeepers are influenced by the hegemony of the social system that they then work to maintain.

Some messages may be selected because they reinforce the status quo, but others may be selected because they point out potential dangers that need to be dealt with if the status quo is to be maintained. This does not mean, however, that gatekeepers will never select messages that are critical of the status quo; in fact, to retain their legitimacy as news organizations, the U.S. media have to be adversarial—within certain ideological bounds. For example, media coverage of the Watergate scandal during the Nixon presidency was highly critical of Richard Nixon and his advisers, but the media did not question the legitimacy of the

American political system; the scandal was framed in terms of the individuals' crimes. As Gitlin (1980) points out, the entire affair ultimately celebrated the American system—it's so good it can survive the crimes of its caretakers.

Thus we find that the forces that Lewin (1951) describes around gates are determined at least in part by culture, societal interests, societal structure, and ideology. If a message is culturally unavailable, it would have a negative force, possibly a strong one. If a message runs counter to established ideology, it might have either a negative or a positive force. Deviant messages might be screened out if they threaten the status quo, suggesting a negative force in front of the gate. On the other hand, deviance might exert a positive influence on a message's selection if the message could signal the need for social "repair." Shoemaker (1984) suggests that deviant ideas are not screened out of the media but are treated in such a way as to delegitimize them. Thus, although deviant messages might have a positive force in front of the gate, once inside the gate, the force could take on negative aspects that would result in the message being shaped as not legitimate.

Note

1. Adams's (1980) conception of boundary roles is only one way in which organizations may communicate with those in the external environment. Eisenberg et al. (1985, pp. 238-243) refer to this as "representative information exchange," because a representative of the organization interacts with those outside the organization. In "institutional information exchange," organizations communicate with each other automatically, as in automatic transactions or sharing of data; no person is directly involved.

4. A New Gatekeeping Model

Figures 4.1, 4.2, and 4.3 summarize and integrate what is known about gatekeeping, based on the theoretical approaches we have

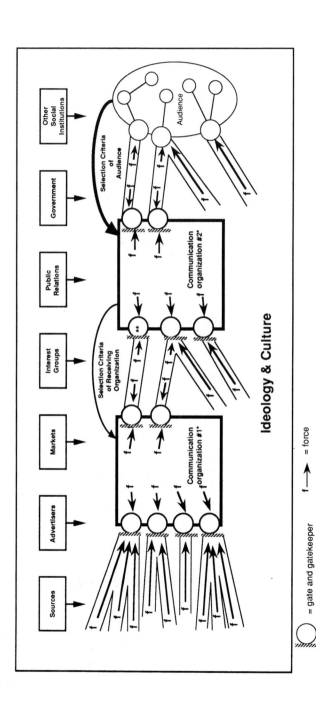

Figure 4.1. Gatekeeping between organizations is embedded in social system ideology and culture and is influenced by social and institutional factors.

NOTE: As an example, communication organizations could include wire services, public relations agencies, television networks, or newspapers.
*See Figure 4.2 for a detailed version of gatekeeping within an organization.
**See Figure 4.3 for a detailed version of gatekeeping within an individual.

discussed. Figures 4.2 and 4.3 are not independent models but represent enlargements of portions of Figure 4.1. The overall process is shown in Figure 4.1 but without detail within communication organizations and within individual gatekeepers. Figure 4.2 shows the gatekeeping processes within a communication organization, and Figure 4.3 shows the intraindividual psychological processes within one gatekeeper. In Figure 4.1 (see Figures 4.2 and 4.3 for more detail), circles represent individual gatekeepers, vertical bars in front of gatekeepers are gates, and the arrows in front of and behind each gate represent the forces that affect a message's entrance into the gate and what happens to it afterward. The large squares are communication organizations, and small rectangles represent social and institutional factors. One or more channels lead to and from each gate and gatekeeper, each carrying one or more messages or potential messages.

The process starts with a variety of potential messages traveling through multiple channels to any of several types of communication organizations, such as a wire service, a public relations agency, a newspaper, or a television network. An organization may have multiple staff members operating in boundary role input positions, each with the power to control which potential messages actually enter the organization and the power to shape the message.

Moving to the organizational enlargement (Figure 4.2), we see that, within a complex organization, the boundary role gatekeepers in charge of inputs may channel selected messages to one or more internal gatekeepers, who may exert their own selection processes and who also may shape the message in a variety of ways. The surviving, shaped messages are then transmitted to boundary role gatekeepers for final shaping, selection, and transmission directly to the audience or to another communication organization (see Figure 4.1). As the feedback loop from organization 2 to organization 1 (and from the audience to organization 2) indicates, selection of messages for outputting is heavily influenced by the selection criteria of the receiver. As Figure 4.2 shows, the gatekeeping processes internal to the organization are embedded in the organization's communication routines and characteristics, which affect the decisions organizational gatekeepers make. Figure 4.2 also provides for the

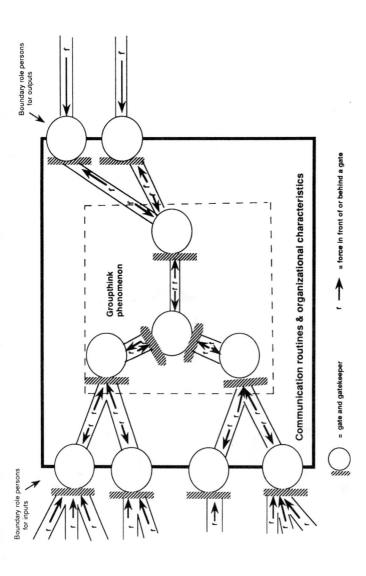

Figure 4.2. Gatekeeping within an organization is embedded in communication organizational characteristics.

NOTE: See Figure 4.3 for intraindividual gatekeeping processes.

73

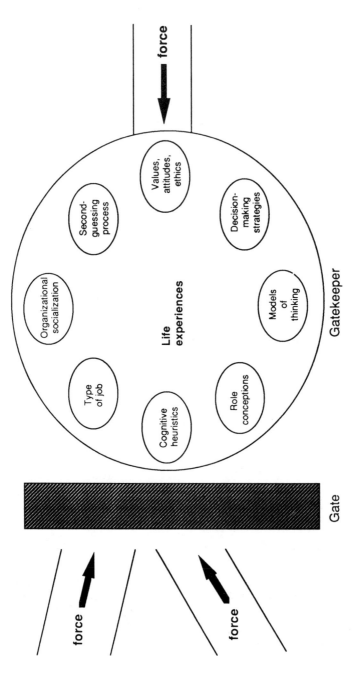

Figure 4.3. Intraindividual gatekeeping processes.

NOTE: Intraindividual-level variables are embedded in life experiences.

"groupthink" phenomenon (Janis, 1983), particularly among socially cohesive groups of gatekeepers.

Figure 4.3 identifies various psychological processes and individual characteristics that can affect the gatekeeping process, including cognitive heuristics, models of thinking, socialization, second-guessing, values, attitudes, decision-making strategies, role conceptions, and type of job. Just as the broader gatekeeping model (Figure 4.1) is embedded in social system ideology and culture, and within-organization gatekeeping (Figure 4.2) is embedded in communication routines and organizational characteristics, individual-level gatekeeping processes (Figure 4.3) are embedded in the individual's life experiences.

Thus we see the complexity of the gatekeeping process. The individual gatekeeper has likes and dislikes, ideas about the nature of his or her job, ways of thinking about a problem, preferred decision-making strategies, and values that all impinge on the decision to reject or select (and shape) a message. But the gatekeeper is not totally free to follow a personal whim; he or she must operate within the constraints of communication routines to do things this way or that. All of this also must occur within the framework of the communication organization, which has its own priorities but also is continuously buffeted by influential forces from outside the organization. And, of course, none of these actors—the individual, the routine, the organization, or the social institution—can escape the fact that it is tied to and draws its sustenance from the social system.

5. Future Research

Even a multiple-level model such as is shown in Figures 4.1 through 4.3 still leaves many questions unanswered. Although the gatekeeping literature covers nearly 50 years and scores of studies, more can be done. This final section will suggest directions for future studies.

First, scholars would be well advised to consider the roles that gatekeeping can play on multiple levels of analysis. Some studies include variables from more than one level—for example, personal attitudes (individual level) with communication routines; this is in principle an advantage because it increases the richness of the study. However, if variables from multiple levels are combined in one analysis, this could confuse interpretation of the results.

Second, the linkages between levels could particularly benefit from study: Exactly what is the mechanism through which social system variables affect social institutions, and how do these influence communication organizations? In what ways do communication organizations and their routines influence gatekeeping processes within individuals?

Third, the relative power of the levels should be addressed. One line of thought holds that individual-level influences are least important, being effectively controlled by communication routines and influences from higher levels. As we indicated earlier, however, some studies (Sasser & Russell, 1972; Stempel, 1985) suggest that communication routines override individual influences in some circumstances but not in others. As Hirsch (1977, p. 21) points out, gatekeeping studies are primarily interested in "subjective bias," and this can operate at more than the individual level of analysis. If an individual gatekeeper wants to base decisions on his or her personal attitudes, to what extent can this be done? How much autonomy and power do individual gatekeepers have to impose their own agendas on media content? What conditions would be conducive to the exercise of personal judgment over more structural constraints?

Fourth, study of the individual needs to progress beyond simple questions of attitudes or bias. We have suggested a variety of intraindividual approaches (e.g., models of thinking, cognitive heuristics, second-guessing, decision making) that could help identify the extent to which individual-level processes are important.

Fifth, the extension of gatekeeping into the higher levels of analysis allows us to use some theoretical approaches that are not generally applied to gatekeeping and presents many ideas for research. The boundary roles perspective (Adams, 1980) seems particularly fruitful, suggesting new interpretations of old studies, as suggested above. If Adams is correct, the wire services may use their own criteria to select input messages but use criteria from the receiving organizations to select outputs. This reverses the assumed causal direction in several gatekeeping studies and suggests that the media get from wire services what they want rather than what the wire services want them to have.

Sixth, studies should do more with the gates themselves and the forces surrounding them. Does the number of items in front of or behind a gate affect the polarity and strength of the force exerted? Must forces always change polarity? Is movement through a gate always unidirectional or could some items move "backward"? What would cause them to do so? Are some gates "lower" than others?

Seventh, the study of gatekeeping ought to be broadened beyond mere selection to the shaping, display, timing, withholding, or repetition of messages (Donohue et al., 1972). We ought to investigate particularly the role of pre- and postgate forces in these processes of nonselection.

Eighth, more can be done with characteristics of the messages. Nisbett and Ross (1980) have suggested that vivid messages would be more likely than pallid messages to pass through a gate, but this idea has not been used in gatekeeping research. We need to progress beyond a categorization of messages (e.g., human interest, economy, international issues) to develop a number of continuous dimensions on which messages can be measured. This will add much to our ability to predict whether and in what form a message will pass through a gate.

Ninth, we might compare the gatekeeping activities of various types of communication organizations, such as television networks and local stations, newspapers, radio stations, advertising agencies, public relations agencies, and magazines. How do communication routines differ? How do the differing goals of these organizations affect inputs and outputs not just in terms of selection but also in terms of how the messages are shaped?

References

Abbott, E. A., & Brassfield, L. T. (1989). Comparing decisions on releases by TV and newspaper gatekeepers. *Journalism Quarterly, 66,* 853-856.

Adams, J. S. (1 80). Interorganizational processes and organizational boundary spanning activities. In B. M. Staw & L. L. Cummings (Eds.), *Research in organizational behavior* (Vol. 2, pp. 321-355). Greenwich, CT: JAI.

Alexander, J. C. (1981). The mass news media in systemic, historical, and comparative perspective. In E. Katz & T. Szecskö (Eds.), *Mass media and social change* (pp. 17-51). Beverly Hills, CA: Sage.

Altschull, H. J. (1984). *Agents of power.* New York: Longman.

Anderson, D. A. (1982). Handling of controversial "merry-go-round" columns. *Journalism Quarterly, 59,* 295-298.

Badii, N., & Ward, W. J. (1980). The nature of news in four dimensions. *Journalism Quarterly, 57,* 243-248.

Bagdikian, B. H. (1983). *The media monopoly.* Boston: Beacon.

Bales, R. F. (1958). Role and role conflict. In E. Maccoby, T. M. Newcomb, & E. L. Hartley (Eds.), *Readings in social psychology* (3rd ed., pp. 437-447). New York: Holt, Rinehart & Winston.

Bales, R. F., Strodtbeck, F. L., Mills, T. M., & Roseborough, M. E. (1951). Channels of communication in small groups. *American Sociological Review, 16,* 461-467.

Bantz, C. R. (1980, November). *Organizing the news: Extending newswork theorizing through Weick's organizing formulation.* Paper presented at the Speech Communication Association Annual Conference, New York.

Bantz, C. R. (1990a). Organizing and enactment: Karl Weick and the production of news. In S. Corman, S. Banks, C. Bantz, & M. Mayer (Eds.), *Foundations of organizational communication: A reader* (pp. 133-141). New York: Longman.

Bantz, C. R. (1990b). Organizational communication, media industries, and mass communication. In J. Anderson (Ed.), *Communication yearbook* (Vol. 13, pp. 502-510). Newbury Park, CA: Sage.

Bantz, C. R., McCorkle, S., & Baade, R. C. (1981). The news factory. In G. C. Wilhoit & H. deBock (Eds.), *Mass communication review yearbook* (Vol. 2, pp. 366-389). Beverly Hills, CA: Sage.

Bass, A. Z. (1969). Refining the "gatekeeper" concept: A UN radio case study. *Journalism Quarterly, 46,* 69-72.

Bavelas, A. (1942). A method for investigating individual and group ideology. *Sociometry, 5,* 371-377.

Bavelas, A. (1948). A mathematical model for group structures. *Applied Anthropology, 7,* 16-30.

Bonn, T. L. (1989). *Heavy traffic & high culture: New American Library as literary gatekeeper in the paperback revolution.* Carbondale: Southern Illinois University Press.

Boorstin, D. J. (1971). From news-gathering to news-making: A flood of pseudo-events. In W. Schramm & D. F. Roberts (Eds.), *The process and effects of mass communication* (pp. 116-150). Urbana: University of Illinois Press.

Breed, W. (1955). Social control in the newsroom: A functional analysis. *Social Forces, 33,* 326-335.

Brown, R. M. (1979). The gatekeeper reassessed: A return to Lewin. *Journalism Quarterly, 56,* 595-601, 679.

Buckalew, J. K. (1969). A Q-analysis of television news editors' decisions. *Journalism Quarterly, 46,* 135-137.

Cantor, M. G. (1980). *Prime-time television: Content and control.* Beverly Hills, CA: Sage.

Cantor, M. G., & Pingree, S. (1983). *The soap opera.* Beverly Hills, CA: Sage.

Chaffee, S. H. (1975). The diffusion of political information. In S. H. Chaffee (Ed.), *Political communication: Issues and strategies for research* (pp. 85-128). Beverly Hills, CA: Sage.

Chibnall, S. (1975). The crime reporter: A study in the production of commercial knowledge. *Sociology, 9,* 49-66.

Chibnall, S. (1977). *Law-and-order news: An analysis of crime reporting in the British press.* London: Tavistock.

Chibnall, S. (1981). The production of knowledge by crime reporters. In S. Cohen & J. Young (Eds.), *The manufacture of news: Deviance, social problems, and the mass media* (pp. 75-97). Beverly Hills, CA: Sage.

Cohen, B. C. (1963). *The press and foreign policy.* Westport, CT: Greenwood.

Cooper, K. (1942). *Barriers down: The story of the news agency epoch.* New York: Farrar & Rinehart.

Crouse, T. (1972). *The boys on the bus: Riding with the campaign press corps.* New York: Random House.

Cutlip, S. M. (1954). Content and flow of AP news—from trunk to TTS to reader. *Journalism Quarterly, 31,* 434-446.

Danielian, L. H., & Reese, S. D. (1989). A closer look at intermedia influences on agenda setting: The cocaine issue of 1986. In P. J. Shoemaker (Ed.), *Communication campaigns about drugs: Government, media, public* (pp. 47-66). Hillsdale, NJ: Lawrence Erlbaum.

Dennis, E. E., & Ismach, A. H. (1981). *Reporting processes and practices.* Belmont, CA: Wadsworth.

Deutschmann, P. J. (1959). *News-page content of twelve metropolitan dailies.* Cincinnati: Scripps Howard Research.

Donohew, L. (1967). Newspaper gatekeepers and forces in the news channel. *Public Opinion Quarterly, 31,* 61-68.

Donohue, G. A., Olien, C. N., & Tichenor, P. J. (1989). Structure and constraints on community newspaper gatekeepers. *Journalism Quarterly, 66,* 807-812, 845.

Donohue, G. A., Tichenor, P. J., & Olien, C. N. (1972). Gatekeeping: Mass media systems and information control. In F. G. Kline & P. J. Tichenor (Eds.), *Current perspectives in mass communication research* (pp. 41-70). Beverly Hills, CA: Sage.

Dyer, C., & Nayman, O. (1977). Under the capitol dome: Relationships between legislators and reporters. *Journalism Quarterly, 54,* 443-453.

Eisenberg, E. M., Farace, R. V., Monge, P. R., Bettinghaus, E. P., Kurchner-Hawkins, R., Miller, K. I., & Rothman, L. (1985). Communication linkages in interorganizational systems: Review and synthesis. In B. Dervin & M. Voigt (Eds.), *Progress in communication sciences* (Vol. 6, pp. 231-262). Norwood, NJ: Ablex.

Ettema, J. S. (1988). *The craft of the investigative journalist*. Evanston, IL: Northwestern University.

Ettema, J. S., & Whitney, D. C., with Wackman, D. B. (1987). Professional mass communicators. In C. R. Berger & S. H. Chaffee (Eds.), *Handbook of communication science* (pp. 747-780). Newbury Park, CA: Sage.

Fensch, T. C. (1977). *Between author and editor: The selected correspondence of John Steinbeck and Pascal Covici, 1945-1952*. Unpublished doctoral dissertation, Syracuse University.

Fink, C. C. (1989, March). How newspapers should handle upscale/downscale conundrum. *Presstime*, pp. 40-41.

Fishbein, M., & Ajzen, I. (1981). Acceptance, yielding and impact: Cognitive processes in persuasion. In R. E. Petty, T. M. Ostrom, & T. C. Brock (Eds.), *Cognitive responses in persuasion* (pp. 339-359). Hillsdale, NJ: Lawrence Erlbaum.

Flegel, R. C., & Chaffee, S. H. (1971). Influences of editors, readers, and personal opinions on reporters. *Journalism Quarterly, 48*, 645-651.

Galtung, J., & Ruge, M. H. (1965). The structure of foreign news. *Journal of Peace Research, 2*, 64-90.

Gandy, O. H., Jr. (1982). *Beyond agenda setting: Information subsidies and public policy*. Norwood, NJ: Ablex.

Gans, H. (1979a). *Deciding what's news*. New York: Pantheon.

Gans, H. J. (1979b, January/February). The messages behind the news. *Columbia Journalism Review*, pp. 40-45.

Garcia, A. (1967). A study of the opinions and attitudes of California's capital correspondents. *Journalism Quarterly, 44*, 330-333.

Gieber, W. (1956). Across the desk: A study of 16 telegraph editors. *Journalism Quarterly, 33*, 423-432.

Gieber, W. (1960). How the "gatekeepers" view local civil liberties news. *Journalism Quarterly, 37*, 199-205.

Gieber, W. (1961). The city hall "beat": A study of reporter and source roles. *Journalism Quarterly, 38*, 289-297.

Gieber, W. (1963, December). "I" am the news. In W. A. Danielson (Ed.), *Paul J. Deutschmann memorial papers in mass communications research* (pp. 9-17). Cincinnati: Scripps-Howard Research.

Gieber, W. (1964). News is what newspapermen make it. In L. A. Dexter & D. M. White (Eds.), *People, society and mass communication*. New York: Free Press.

Gieber, W., & Johnson, W. (1961). The city hall "beat": A study of reporter and source roles. *Journalism Quarterly, 38*, 289-297.

Gitlin, T. (1980). *The whole world is watching*. Berkeley: University of California Press.

Gold, D., & Simmons, J. L. (1965). News selection patterns among Iowa dailies. *Public Opinion Quarterly, 29*, 425-430.

Goldenberg, E. N. (1975). *Making the papers: The access of resource-poor groups to the metropolitan press*. Lexington, MA: Lexington Books.

Golding, P. (1981). The missing dimensions: News media and the management of social change. In E. Katz & T. Szecskö (Eds.), *Mass media and social change* (pp. 63-81). Beverly Hills, CA: Sage.

Gramsci, A. (1971). *Selections from the Prison Notebooks of Antonio Gramsci* (Q. Hoare & G. N. Smith, Eds.). New York: International Publishers.

Greenberg, B. S. (1964). Person-to-person communication in the diffusion of news events. *Journalism Quarterly, 41*, 489-494.

Greenberg, B. S., & Tannenbaum, P. H. (1962). Communicator performance under cognitive stress. *Journalism Quarterly, 39*, 169-178.

Grey, D. L. (1966). Decision-making by a reporter under deadline pressure. *Journalism Quarterly, 43,* 419-428.

Halloran, J. D., Elliott, P., & Murdock, G. (1970). *Demonstrations and communication: A case study.* Baltimore: Penguin.

Hardt, H. (1979). *Social theories of the press: Early German & American perspectives.* Beverly Hills, CA: Sage.

Harmon, M. D. (1989). Mr. Gates goes electronic: The what and why questions in local TV news. *Journalism Quarterly, 66,* 857-863.

Harriss, J., Leiter, K., & Johnson, S. (1977). *The complete reporter.* New York: Macmillan.

Hewes, D. E., & Graham, M. L. (1989). Second-guessing theory: Review and extension. In J. A. Anderson (Ed.), *Communication yearbook* (Vol. 12, pp. 213-248). Newbury Park, CA: Sage.

Hickey, J. R. (1966). *The effects of information control on perceptions of centrality.* Unpublished doctoral dissertation, University of Wisconsin.

Hickey, J. R. (1968). The effects of information control on perceptions of centrality. *Journalism Quarterly, 45,* 49-54.

Hirsch, P. M. (1970). *The structure of the popular music industry.* Ann Arbor: University of Michigan, Institute for Social Research.

Hirsch, P. M. (1977). Occupational, organizational and institutional models in mass media research: Toward an integrated framework. In P. M. Hirsch, P. V. Miller, & F. G. Kline (Eds.), *Strategies for communication research.* Beverly Hills, CA: Sage.

Hirsch, P. M. (1981). Institutional functions of elite and mass media. In E. Katz & T. Szecskö (Eds.), *Mass media and social change* (pp. 187-200). Beverly Hills, CA: Sage.

Homans, G. C. (1950). *The human group.* New York: Harcourt, Brace & World.

Izard, R. S., Culbertson, H. M., & Lambert, D. A. (1973). *Fundamentals of news reporting.* Dubuque, IA: Kendall/Hunt.

Jablin, F. M. (1982). Organizational communication: An assimilation approach. In M. E. Roloff & C. R. Berger (Eds.), *Social cognition and communication* (pp. 255-286). Beverly Hills, CA: Sage.

Janis, I. L. (1983). *Group think: Psychological studies of policy decisions and fiascoes.* Boston: Houghton Mifflin.

Johnstone, J. W. C., Slawski, E. J., & Bowman, W. W. (1972). The professional values of American newsmen. *Public Opinion Quarterly, 36,* 522-540.

Jones, R. L., Troldahl, V. C., & Hvistendahl, J. K. (1961). News selection patterns from a state TTS wire. *Journalism Quarterly, 38,* 303-312.

Judd, R. P. (1961). The newspaper reporter in a suburban city. *Journalism Quarterly, 38,* 35-42.

Kahneman, D., Slovic, P., & Tversky, A. (Eds.). (1982). *Judgment under uncertainty: Heuristics and biases.* Cambridge: Cambridge University Press.

Kerrick, J. S., Anderson, T. E., & Swales, L. B. (1964). Balance and the writer's attitude in news stories and editorials. *Journalism Quarterly, 41,* 207-215.

Kessler, L. (1989). Women's magazines' coverage of smoking related health hazards. *Journalism Quarterly, 66,* 316-322, 445.

Lang, K., & Lang, G. E. (1953). The unique perspective of television and its effect: A pilot study. *American Sociological Review, 18,* 3-12.

Larsen, O. N., & Hill, R. J. (1956). Mass media and interpersonal communication in the diffusion of a news event. *American Sociological Review, 19,* 426-433.

Lasswell, H. D. (1971). The structure and function of communication in society. In W. Schramm & D. F. Roberts (Eds.), *The process and effects of mass*

82

communication (pp. 84-99). Urbana: University of Illinois Press. (Reprinted from *The communication of ideas*, edited by L. Bryson, 1948, New York: Institute for Religious and Social Studies)

Lazare, D. (1989, May/June). Vanity fare. *Columbia Journalism Review*, pp. 6, 8.

Lewin, K. (1933). Environmental forces in child behavior and development. In C. Murchison (Ed.), *Handbook of child psychology*. Worchester, MA: Clark University Press.

Lewin, K. (1935). *A dynamic theory of personality: Selected papers* (D. K. Adams & K. E. Zener, Trans.). New York: McGraw-Hill.

Lewin, K. (1943). Forces behind food habits and methods of change. In *The problem of changing food habits* (Bulletin No. 108 of the National Research Council, pp. 35-65). Baltimore: Lord Baltimore Press.

Lewin, K. (1946). Action research and minority problems. *Journal of Social Issues, 2*, 34-46.

Lewin, K. (1947a). Frontiers in group dynamics: Concept, method and reality in science; social equilibria and social change. *Human Relations, 1*, 5-40.

Lewin, K. (1947b). Frontiers in group dynamics: II. Channels of group life; social planning and action research. *Human Relations, 1*, 143-153.

Lewin, K. (1951). *Field theory in social science: Selected theoretical papers*. New York: Harper.

Luttbeg, N. R. (1983a). News consensus: Do U.S. newspapers mirror society's happenings? *Journalism Quarterly, 60*, 484-488, 578.

Luttbeg, N. R. (1983b). Proximity does not assure newsworthiness. *Journalism Quarterly, 60*, 731-732.

MacDougall, A. K. (1988). Boring from within the bourgeois press. Part one. *Monthly Review, 40*(7), 13-24.

Marrow, A. J. (1969). *The practical theorist: The life and work of Kurt Lewin*. New York: Basic Books.

McCombs, M. E., & Shaw, D. L. (1976). Structuring the "unseen environment." *Journal of Communication, 26*, 18-22.

McLeod, J. M., & Chaffee, S. H. (1973). Interpersonal approaches to communication research. *American Behavioral Scientist, 16*, 469-499.

McNelly, J. T. (1959). Intermediary communicators in the international flow of news. *Journalism Quarterly, 36*, 23-26.

McQuail, D., & Windahl, S. (1981). *Communication models for the study of mass communications*. New York: Longman.

Miller, A., Goldenberg, E., & Erbring, L. (1979). Typeset politics: Impact of newspapers on public confidence. *American Political Science Review, 73*, 67-83.

Molotch, H., & Lester, M. (1974). News as purposive behavior: On the strategic use of routine events, accidents, and scandals. *American Sociological Review, 39*, 101-112.

Mulder, M. (1960). The power variable in communication experiments. *Human Relations, 13*, 241-257.

Newcomb, T. M. (1953). An approach to the study of communicative acts. *Psychological Review, 60*, 393-404.

Nisbett, R., & Ross, L. (1980). *Human inference: Strategies and shortcomings of social judgment*. New York: Prentice-Hall.

Noelle-Neumann, E. (1980). Mass media and social·change in developed societies. In G. C. Wilhoit & H. deBock (Eds.), *Mass communication review yearbook* (Vol. 1, pp. 657-678). Beverly Hills, CA: Sage.

O'Sullivan, T., Hartley, J., Saunders, D., & Fiske, J. (Eds.). (1983). *Key concepts in communication*. New York: Methuen.

Pool, I. D. S., & Shulman, I. (1959). Newsmen's fantasies, audiences, and newswriting. *Public Opinion Quarterly, 23*, 145-158.

Ranney, A. (1983). *Channels of power: The impact of television on American politics.* New York: Basic Books.

Reese, S. D., & Danielian, L. H. (1989). Intermedia influence and the drug issue: Converging on cocaine. In P. J. Shoemaker (Ed.), *Communication campaigns about drugs: Government, media, public* (pp. 29-46). Hillsdale, NJ: Lawrence Erlbaum.

Riffe, D., Ellis, B., Rogers, M. K., Van Ommeren, R. L., & Woodman, K. A. (1986). Gatekeeping and the network news mix. *Journalism Quarterly, 63*, 315-321.

Rivers, W. L. (1965). *The opinionmakers.* Boston: Beacon.

Rosten, L. C. (1937). *The Washington correspondents.* New York: Arno.

Ryan, M. (1982). Evaluating scholarly manuscripts in journalism and mass communication. *Journalism Quarterly, 59*, 273-285.

Sasser, E. L., & Russell, J. T. (1972). The fallacy of news judgment. *Journalism Quarterly, 49*, 280-284.

Schramm, W. (1949a). The nature of news. *Journalism Quarterly, 26*, 259-269.

Schramm, W. (1949b). The gatekeeper: A memorandum. In W. Schramm (Ed.), *Mass communications* (pp. 175-177). Urbana: University of Illinois Press.

Schramm, W. (1963). The challenge to communication research. In R. O. Nafziger & D. M. White (Eds.), *Introduction to mass communications research* (pp. 3-31). Baton Rouge: Louisiana State University Press.

Shoemaker, P. J. (1984). Media coverage of deviant political groups. *Journalism Quarterly, 61*, 66-75, 82.

Shoemaker, P. J., Chang, T. K., & Brendlinger, N. (1987). Deviance as a predictor of newsworthiness: Coverage of international events in the U.S. media. In M. McLaughlin (Ed.), *Communication yearbook* (Vol. 10, pp. 348-365). Newbury Park, CA: Sage.

Shoemaker, P. J., Danielian, L. H., & Brendlinger, N. (in press). Deviant acts, risky business, and U.S. interests: The newsworthiness of world events. *Journalism Quarterly.*

Shoemaker, P. J., with Mayfield, E. K. (1987). Building a theory of news content [Monograph, entire issue]. *Journalism Monographs, 103.*

Shoemaker, P. J., & Reese, S. D. (1991). *Mediating the message: Theories of influences on mass media content.* New York: Longman.

Sigal, L. V. (1973). *Reporters and officials: The organization and politics of newsmaking.* Lexington, MA: D. C. Heath.

Snider, P. B. (1967). "Mr. Gates" revisited: A 1966 version of the 1949 case study. *Journalism Quarterly, 44*, 419-427.

Snodgrass, J. G., Levy-Berger, G., & Hayden, M. (1985). *Human experimental psychology.* New York: Oxford University Press.

Stempel, G. H., III. (1959). Uniformity of wire content in six Michigan dailies. *Journalism Quarterly, 36*, 45-48, 120.

Stempel, G. H., III. (1962). Content patterns of small and metropolitan dailies. *Journalism Quarterly, 39*, 88-91.

Stempel, G. H., III. (1985). Gatekeeping: The mix of topics and the selection of stories. *Journalism Quarterly, 62*, 791-796, 815.

Stempel, G. H., III. (1989). Content analysis. In G. H. Stempel III & B. H. Westley (Eds.), *Research methods in mass communication* (pp. 124-136). Englewood Cliffs, NJ: Prentice-Hall.

Stephens, M. (1980). *Broadcast news.* New York: Holt, Rinehart & Winston.

84

Stewart, P. L., & Cantor, M. G. (1982). Introduction. In P. L. Stewart & M. G. Cantor (Eds.), *Varieties of work*. Beverly Hills, CA: Sage.

Tankard, J. W., Jr., Middleton, K., & Rimmer, T. (1979). Compliance with American Bar Association fair trial-free press guidelines. *Journalism Quarterly, 56*, 464-468.

Tichenor, P. J., Olien, C. N., Donohue, G. A., & Griswold, W. F., Jr. (1986). *Social change and gatekeeper change: Opinions of community editors, 1965-85.* Paper presented to the American Association for Public Opinion Research.

Todd, R. (1983). New York Times advisories and national/international news selection. *Journalism Quarterly, 60*, 705-708, 676.

Tuchman, G. (1972). Objectivity as strategic ritual: An examination of newsmen's notions of objectivity. *American Journal of Sociology, 77*, 660-679.

Tuchman, G. (1974). Making news by doing work: Routinizing the unexpected. *American Journal of Sociology, 79*, 110-131.

Tuchman, G. (1981). Myth and the consciousness industry: A new look at the effects of the mass media. In E. Katz & T. Szecskö (Eds.), *Mass media and social change* (pp. 83-100). Beverly Hills, CA: Sage.

Tunstall, J. (1971). *Journalists at work*. London: Constable.

Weaver, D. H., & Wilhoit, G. C. (1986). *The American journalist*. Bloomington: Indiana University Press.

Webb, E. J., & Salancik, J. R. (1965). Notes on the sociology of knowledge. *Journalism Quarterly, 42*, 595-596.

Weick, K. (1979). *The social psychology of organizing*. Reading, MA: Addison-Wesley.

Westley, B. H. (1953). *News editing*. Cambridge, MA: Houghton-Mifflin.

Westley, B. H., & MacLean, M. S., Jr. (1957). A conceptual model for communications research. *Journalism Quarterly, 34*, 31-38.

White, D. M. (1950). The "gate keeper": A case study in the selection of news. *Journalism Quarterly, 27*, 383-390.

Whitney, D. C. (1981). Information overload in the newsroom. *Journalism Quarterly, 58*, 69-76, 161.

Whitney, D. C., & Becker, L. B. (1982). "Keeping the gates" for gatekeepers: The effects of wire news. *Journalism Quarterly, 59*, 60-65.

Williams, R. (1977). *Marxism and literature*. New York: Oxford University Press.

Wolfsfeld, G. (1984). Collective political action and media strategy. *Journal of Conflict Resolution, 28*, 363-381.

Woodward, B., & Bernstein, C. (1974). *All the president's men*. New York: Simon & Schuster.

Wright, C. R. (1986). *Mass communication: A sociological perspective*. New York: Random House.

Wright, P., & Barbour, F. (1976). The relevance of decision process models in structuring persuasive messages. In M. Ray & S. Ward (Eds.), *Communicating with consumers*. Beverly Hills, CA: Sage.

Author Index

About the Author

Pamela J. Shoemaker is the Director of the School of Journalism at Ohio State University. Formerly, she was Associate Professor of Journalism at the University of Texas at Austin. She is the author (with Stephen D. Reese) of *Mediating the Message: Theories of Influences on Mass Media Content* and the editor of *Communicating Campaigns About Drugs: Government, Media, Public*. Her research has included the role of deviance in the newsworthiness concept and the ways in which deviant political groups are portrayed by the mass media. She is an associate editor of *Journalism Quarterly* as well as the 1990 recipient of the Association for Education in Journalism and Mass Communication's Krieghbaum Under-40 Award for outstanding achievement in research, teaching, and public service. She holds a Ph.D. in mass communication from the University of Wisconsin–Madison.